1866 - 1991

125th

ANNIVERSARY

IN CONDOR COUNTRY

*A Portrait of a Landscape,
Its Denizens, and Its Defenders*

DAVID DARLINGTON

An Owl Book

HENRY HOLT AND COMPANY
New York

Published by Henry Holt and Company, Inc.,
115 West 18th Street, New York, New York 10011.
Published in Canada by Fitzhenry and Whiteside Limited,
195 Allstate Parkway, Markham, Ontario L3R 4T8.

Library of Congress Cataloging-in-Publication Data
Darlington, David.
In condor country: a portrait of a landscape, its denizens, and
its defenders / David Darlington. — 1st Owl ed.
p.   cm.
"An Owl book."
Originally published: Houghton Mifflin, 1987.
Includes bibliographical references and index.
1. California condor.   2. Birds, Protection of — California — San
Luis Obispo County.   3. Natural history — California — San Luis Obispo
County.   4. McMillan, Eben.   5. McMillan, Ian I.   6. San Luis Obispo
County (Calif.) — Biography.   7. Birds — California — San Luis Obispo
County.   8. Ranchers — California — Biography.   9. Conservationists —
California — Biography.   I. Title.
QL696.F33D37   1991
333.95'8'0979478 — dc20   91-14790
                                                              CIP

ISBN 0-8050-1750-X (An Owl Book: pbk.)

Henry Holt books are available at special discounts
for bulk purchases for sales promotions, premiums,
fund-raising, or educational use. Special editions
or book excerpts can also be created to specification.
For details contact:
Special Sales Director, Henry Holt and Company, Inc.,
115 West 18th Street, New York, New York 10011.

First published in hardcover by Houghton Mifflin
Company in 1987.

First Owl Book Edition — 1991

Printed in the United States of America
Recognizing the importance of preserving the written word,
Henry Holt and Company, Inc., by policy, prints all of its
first editions on acid-free paper. ∞

1   3   5   7   9   10   8   6   4   2

To *Carol Cleveland*
and
In Memoriam
Bethany Korwin-Pawlowska
A lover of raptors
1954–1986

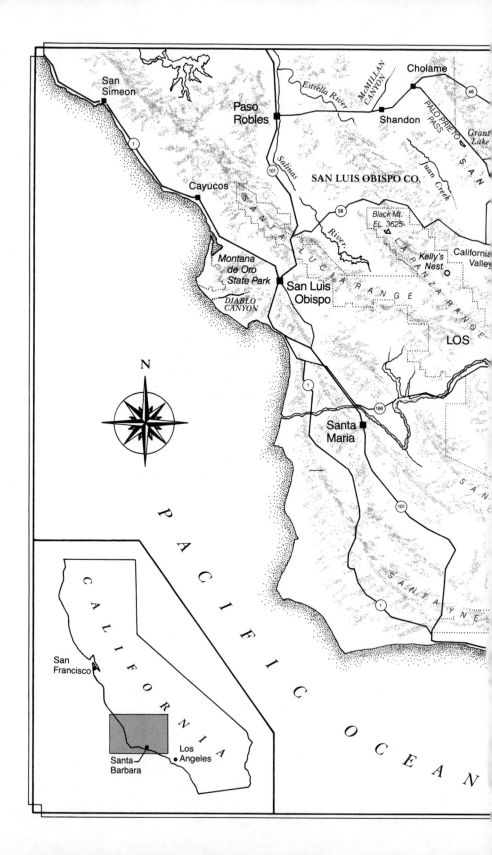

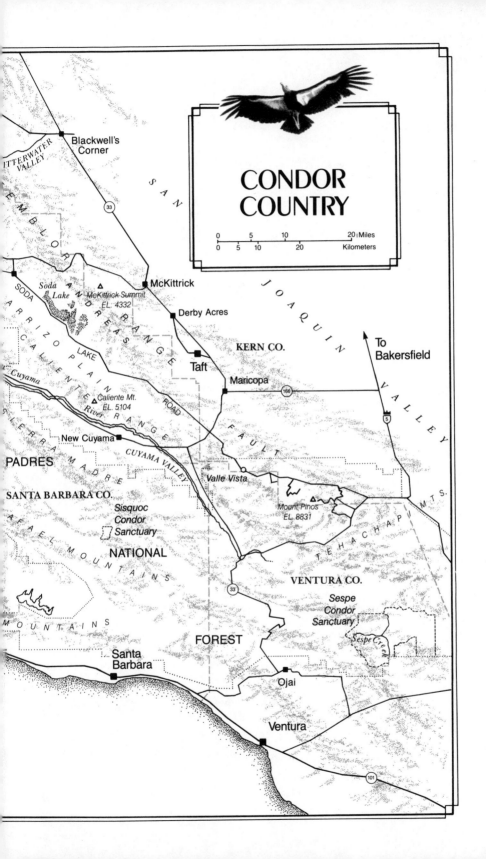

CONDOR COUNTRY

0   5   10   20 Miles
0 5 10   20   Kilometers

ITTERWATER VALLEY

Blackwell's Corner

33

S A N

J O A Q U I N

To
Bakersfield

TEMBLOR

RANGE

Soda Lake

McKittrick

McKittrick Summit
EL. 4332

Derby Acres

KERN CO.

Taft

Maricopa

166

5

V A L L E Y

ANDREAS

ARRIZO PLAIN

LAKE

CALIENTE

△ Caliente Mt.
EL. 5104

RANGE

ROAD

New Cuyama

CUYAMA VALLEY

Cuyama River

SODA

SIERRA

MADRE

FAULT

PADRES

SANTA BARBARA CO.

Sisquoc
Condor
Sanctuary

NATIONAL

Valle Vista

Mount Pinos
EL. 8831

△

VENTURA CO.

Sespe
Condor
Sanctuary

Sespe Creek

T E H A C H A P I   MTS.

AFAEL

MOUNTAINS

MOUNTAINS

FOREST

33

Santa
Barbara

Ojai

Ventura

101

The disappearance of plants and animal species without visible cause, despite efforts to protect them, and the irruption of others as pests despite efforts to control them, must, in the absence of simpler explanations, be regarded as symptoms of sickness in the land organism. . . . The practices we now call conservation are, to a large extent, local alleviations of biotic pain. They are necessary, but they must not be confused with cures. The art of land doctoring is being practiced with vigor, but the science of land health is yet to be born.

Aldo Leopold
A Sand County Almanac

IN CONDOR COUNTRY

WHEN EBEN MCMILLAN first moved to his ranch in eastern San Luis Obispo County, California, big shadows would cross the lawn while he and his family were having lunch. Everybody would stop eating, run outside, and — if the shadow was still there — see a black condor against the blue sky. ("I'd always watch a condor first and worry about other things later," Eben explains, with regard to lunch.) Forty years ago, days that presented opportunities for condor-watching in that region were more common than those that didn't. If you were doing work that required you to look up — drilling a well, say, and checking to keep the cable from going slack — you'd see condors almost daily. If you heard an airplane and turned your gaze skyward, you were liable to see a condor too. During the sixties, when Eben and his brother Ian were conducting a condor survey for the National Aububon Society, Eben found a dead cat in the road and took it up on a hill behind his house, advising his wife, Gladys, to keep an eye out for eagles. Later that day, Gladys saw nine condors on the carcass — more than today's total population of wild California condors.

Eben thinks that condors were "doing good" then. "In forty-six there were about sixty birds, and they were pumping three or four a year into the population," he says. "But after my brother and I did that study, it began to seem that something unusual was happening." "Something unusual" was drastic decline: when Ian saw a condor circling near his house in 1984, it was the first one he had spotted in seventeen years.

Of course, it is hardly unusual *not* to see a California condor. While its sighting is facilitated by the fact that it is the largest land bird in North America, it is also the rarest, and it was extinct throughout most of the continent by the time the McMillan brothers saw their first one. When Europeans settled the West Coast in the eighteenth century, condors were common from Baja California to British Columbia; and fossil remains of *Gymnogyps amplus,* a Pleistocene ancestor of the condor we know today, have been found as far away as Florida. These ancient origins have supported the popular notion that the condor is a prehistoric relic whose disappearance is inevitable in the path of modern civilization, but in fact the oldest fossil remains of *Gymnogyps californianus* — the California condor — are younger than those of man. Condors did once depend on the wild carrion of deer, elk, antelope, and whale, but in modern times they have fed as well on the carcasses of domestic cattle and sheep. Condors shy away from civilization, but they aren't inherently incompatible with it; today a favorite California condor flyway follows U.S. Interstate 5. "It is barbarism, not civilization, that has destroyed the condor," Ian McMillan once wrote. "Barbarism with guns, poison, the bulldozer and ruinous economic growth."

The last refuge of the condor is a horseshoe-shaped range of mountains surrounding the southern part of California's San Joaquin Valley. It has been Eben and Ian McMillan's home for eighty years. I met the two of them in 1980, when I drove down to Santa Barbara from my home in Oakland for a round-table discussion about condor preservation. At the time, the captive propagation plan now being implemented by the National Audubon Society and the U.S. Fish and Wildlife Service was still under debate, and the biologists who began it were meeting their "opposition" — people from environmental groups like Friends of the Earth and the Sierra Club, who held that the captive breeding of condors could hasten rather than prevent the demise of the species. Aside from the fabled sensitivity of condors and the philosophical question of whether a cage-raised bird, even if successfully released, can ever be called wild, the environmentalists maintained that the Condor Recovery Program was only addressing symptoms of the birds' real problem. What malfunction of the environment, after all, was killing condors off? And what's the use of releasing captive-bred birds into a still-unhealthy habitat?

The scientists putting together the program — John Ogden of Audubon and Noel Snyder of the USFWS — met these protestations with chuckling and head-shaking. They said that they had found condors to be tough, curious, resilient animals. They agreed that the habitat had not been adequately maintained, but they suggested that that was the task of the U.S. Forest Service; they themselves were wildlife specialists, employed by other agencies. They insisted that many crucial questions about condor mortality could be answered only through radiotelemetry, which would require at least trapping the birds; having struggled on foot over the area's practically impassable topography, they were unreceptive to criticism from people who had never even visited the habitat. When they met with so little responsiveness, the environmentalists' frustration led them to press the scientists in ever more unctuous tones; personal insults were eventually delivered and apologies demanded. The meeting ultimately seemed to fit the unfortunate stereotype of environmental confrontations: a standoff between bureaucrats and elitists.

Amid this atmosphere of defensiveness and stridency, the person who struck me as possessing the most reasoned, forceful, and far-sighted voice was an elderly rancher in a neat cowboy shirt who had attended the meeting independently to argue against captive breeding. "I think we can get along without condors," he said, "but we can't get along without taking care of the environment. The condor is just a warning signal — if you're driving your car and the oil light comes on, you know you better stop her right there and not go any farther until you know what's wrong. Well, the condor is our shining red light." The man was Eben McMillan.

I ran into him again later that spring, at a hearing where the California Fish and Game Commission, to no one's surprise, approved the captive breeding of condors. Eben invited me and a young Sierra Club activist named Mark Palmer to visit his ranch when the meeting was over. Palmer had never been there before, but he told me he'd had dreams about the place; Eben's relationship to young environmentalists is that of a light to moths, and his ranch represents a pit stop to people who need to refuel their ideals. In the lush spring of that year, it did seem like a dream: the wheat and willows were green and waving, and the tamarisk tree below the house was blooming pink. The yard was filled with quail and rabbits, finches were nesting on the front porch, and Eben had a "pet" (that is, uncaged) roadrunner to whom he fed a live mouse each morning. This "ranch," it seemed, was really a front for a wildlife refuge.

Palmer and I followed Eben on foot into the backcountry in order to look at a defunct condor nest site in the pitted face of a cliff. Eben at the time was seventy-two; Palmer and I ate his dust. On the way home we ran into Ian, wearing a cowboy hat and a bandanna, poised on his horse against the bare hills at sunset. He was then recovering from a recent heart attack and didn't say much except, "It's good to know that the young people are carrying it on." Having been under the common impression that the environmental battle is waged primarily by young people (and that old ranchers are their inherent enemies), I was delighted to realize that the McMillan brothers had been arguing for nature long before Palmer and I had come into the world.

I began to correspond with Eben after that. In the summer I was bothered by a raccoon that was getting into my garbage, so I called the county animal control department, which gave me a trap; that night I heard a slap in the dark, and when I shone my flashlight through the window saw a masked face in the cage. The next morning I went out to look at the coon, which regarded me silently from a position on its back. It had tried to claw its way out of the cage, and its forelegs were bloody. The county came and picked the animal up. Regretting the incident, I wrote to Eben, asking for advice on how to deal with such problems. He responded:

Your raccoon experience is normal in the behavior of any mammal driven to survive in an environment where it has never evolved the capacity to exist on its own terms. Such an individual is probably the fringe member who, rather than being directly crowded out of existence by natural roles, still hangs on where its race or species has no chance of ever establishing itself as an integral part of the fauna of your city. Without your garbage can, that individual would surely have left no genes to carry on. It's nature's continuity that one must concern himself with, and not waste time trying to save an individual that is marked for the category of cast-off. . . . Don't overlook a good, fat coon in the plan to keep protein intake high. Mississippi raccoons dare not go carelessly about in the interest of their meat, which, a Southerner will admit, is not bad victuals.

Soon after that, the condor scientists — without proper legal authorization — entered a nest cave to weigh and measure a condor chick, one of two then known to exist. The nestling died from shock, terminating (for the time being) the captive breeding program. When I heard what had happened I called Eben, who said, "They have to be either ignorant or arrogant. I don't see how anybody in their right mind would get themselves into a situation like that at a time like this. You couldn't've got me in there if I'd been drunk for a week. Ninety percent of the testimony warned that we don't know how condors will react to being handled." When I told him that Ogden, the Audubon biologist who oversaw the operation, had handled hundreds of wood storks in their nests without mishap, Eben answered, "I don't care how experienced you are. Anybody who knows anything about animals knows you can't tell from one to the next how they're going to react. Biologists are narrow specialists, and they don't necessarily have a better overview than anybody else. I might have been able to accept this captive breeding proposal if I thought it was the final step, but I think it's part of a trend — toward professionalization of the outdoors."

The red light that the chick's death represented shone relatively briefly. A new permit to trap condors was issued the following year, and over the next four, every chick and every egg of the species *Gymnogyps californianus* was removed from the wild. In the five years following the death of the chick — the first five years of captive propagation — the wild condor population shrank by 85 percent: where there had been thirty birds in the wild when the program began, by 1985 there were four.

I visited Eben at irregular intervals during this chain of events. None of it surprised him. He was sure that several breeding pairs of condors had broken up as a direct result of the nest invasions by the scientists. In his opinion, raising birds in captivity — as opposed to preserving them in the wild — had always been the primary goal of the Condor Recovery Program, which he referred to as "a good example of how not to conduct a biological research project."

Eben declared, "In any other line of endeavor, by now we would have said, 'Wait a minute, fellas — stop in tomorrow and pick up your checks.' The problem with an awful lot of researchers is that they attribute an excessive amount of ignorance to animals. In many ways a bird is smarter than the person who's watching it. We don't understand animal reactions because we're civilized — we've lost our feeling for those emotions. As human beings we're dependent on our voices, but one animal will pass word of danger or safety to another just by its behavior. We have a parental attitude toward animals, and when we see things happen that are debilitating to them, we think it's our responsibility to help. But we need to learn to stay away. If you give animals half a chance, they'll flourish. The way to take care of wildlife is to take care of the environment."

Any species with a population as low as that of the California condor is no longer an important component of its ecosystem. Everyone involved with the condor agrees that its primary importance in this day and age is symbolic: it is less an endangered species than an embodiment of *all* endangered species. It is often referred to as a miner's canary — when it stops singing, it's time to get out of the shaft. Since the beginning of the European settlement of North America, more than five hundred species and subspecies of plants and animals on this continent have become extinct, and at the present rate — according to the *Global 2000 Report to the President,* commissioned during the Carter administration — the world will have lost somewhere between six hundred thousand and one million of its plant and animal species by the turn of the coming century (along with one third of its agricultural land and two thirds of its forests). The condor is only the most immediate index in this trend, but the course taken with it has been a preview of how conservationists will meet this crisis.

Other birds in recent times have been as endangered as the condor, but none has possessed the portfolio of attributes that has made this one such a conspicuous totem. Its size sets it apart right away; with a wingspread of nine and a half feet, condors can soar for more than an hour without flapping their wings. When the birds do beat them, the sound is audible a half mile away, and when they glide by at close range, the wind in their feathers makes a whistling, musical sound. The imagery of extinction is augmented by the bird's being a vulture. And there's its proximity to Los Angeles — circling silently above a metropolis founded on fossil fuel, this prehistoric raptor almost seems ready to feed on the forces that have fed on it.

This fact — that it's the *California* condor — seems to carry a special piquancy. California is America in microcosm: a despoiled Eden and world-famous focus of aspiration and disillusion, where the best and worst elements of modern life are on daily exhibit. Somehow it's fitting that this largest of land birds should be struggling for survival in this most coveted and controversial of human habitats. While it might not have been determined solely because of its symbolic aptness, the condor's choice of a place to make a last stand was not arrived at accidentally. At the beginning of this century, the ornithologist William Leon Dawson wrote: "For me the heart of California lies in the condor country. And for me the heart of mystery, of wonder, and of desire lies with the California condor." Given the highly symbolic nature not merely of the condor but of its habitat, it seemed to me that time spent with Eben and Ian McMillan would offer glimpses not only into the continent's past but into the earth's future. By extension and no great stretch of the imagination, the entire planet is condor country.

The dividing line between northern and southern California is a matter of continual debate, but the McMillans' home ground — the area surrounding the tiny towns of Shandon and Cholame — qualifies as such in a specific way: it's almost exactly halfway between San Francisco and Los Angeles. An arid region of high, rolling grassland between the Coast Range and the San Joaquin Valley, it resembles the California of popular imagination in no way whatsoever. The sheer dryness of the region — the Santa Lucia Mountains bar the cool ocean breezes of summer and retard the moisture-bearing winds of winter — makes it one of the most sparsely settled areas of the state. In the rainy season, from November through April, the hills exude the color of emeralds. The rest of the year they're as dry and brown as grocery bags, parched by hundred-degree heat. The average rainfall on Eben's ranch is nine inches per year; 50 miles to the west, on the coast, it's thirty-five; 20 miles to the east, it's four. Rainfall flowing east from the highest point on Eben's property goes into the San Joaquin Valley; water that flows west from the same point winds up in the Salinas. The dry tule fog of the interior and the wet fog of the coast collide near Eben's ranch, resulting in spectacular aeromechanical displays.

In many ways, then, the McMillans live in a boundary region, on a biotic line between coastal and desert climates. The line fluctuates and changes annually, according to the weather. Coastal species like the gray fox, the scrub jay, and the western bluebird proliferate in wet years, whereas desert species like the kit fox and roadrunner increase their numbers in dry ones. Some plants that restrict themselves to eastern or western California live side by side only in this part of the state. From a car the country seems deceptively barren: biologists have visited Eben and set out thirty traps in the evening, hoping to collect one or two specimens; in the morning, every trap has been sprung. "The coast has its poundage in large animals," Eben explains. "The desert has it in *millions* of small animals. The amount of life out there is beyond expectation." The result — especially in the silent, oak-dotted uplands and foothills of the Caliente and La Panza mountains, silent places where condors once roosted — is indeed a feeling of mystery, a sense that things are going on that human beings will never know.

In the midst of this empty and enigmatic landscape, Eben's ranch is, by his own definition, an oasis. It contains more than two dozen species of trees — among them willow, cottonwood, sycamore, juniper, tamarisk, box elder, cherry plum, fig, olive, Italian cypress, blue and valley oak, Delicious and Gravenstein apple, digger, Coulter, Monterey, and Torrey pine — most of which he planted himself. Around his house is an apron of thick green grass that, brushed back by hand, holds its shape like the coat of an animal. The house itself sits on the side of a small hill, looking across barley and wheat fields toward the dark, distant line of the San Andreas Fault. Two plate glass windows come together on the northeast corner of the house, above the intersection of Eben's dirt driveway and the Gillis Canyon Road ("Impassable During Wet Weather"). The road disappears around an S-curve at the bottom of a hillside that lights up at sunset, looming like a tidal wave, threatening to engulf the house.

Eben eats his meals by this window, in front of a black-and-white television set that Gladys turns on in the morning and evening for the news. Eben seldom pays attention to the TV except to give a guttural laugh at a pompous public official. "I get too personally involved in television," he admits. "As soon as they start those ads, I know they're taking me for an idiot." Instead, he watches his window; every day there's a wake-up program, a matinee, and a dinner show. A vertical post in the garden welcomes a rotating variety of birds throughout the day. Hummingbirds dart around the "red-hot poker" plant, and roadrunners harass the cottontail rabbits — several of which are usually on the lawn, catapulting around like mechanical toys, feeding in the last light, their ears incandescent. If there are grasshoppers in the mint bush, starlings hover over it like helicopters, emulating the hummingbirds. The window assumes the aspect of a terrarium — a glassed-off landscape for nature study, extending in this case to all outdoors.

"Our presence discourages predators, which allows wildlife to build up numbers far beyond what they'd be if we weren't here," Eben says. "One thing we've learned is that you can't look directly at wildlife; in nature, the only reason one animal stares at another is if it's interested in eating it. But if you just go about your business, they'll accept you the way they would a cow or a horse. We used to have a bobcat hanging around here, and when Gladys was out mowing the lawn he'd just sit there with kind of a benevolent look on his face. But as soon as a stranger's car came up the road, he became a different animal. Wild animals can be compatible with humans, but you have to know what you can do and what you can't."

The only animals Eben says he "discourages" are house-cats, English sparrows, and starlings. Said discouragement generally occurs in conjunction with a .410 shotgun that he keeps by the barn door. Like a Latin American general, he occasionally executes a random starling as an example to the rest of the population. The unlucky targets stay where they drop, rotting in view of other starlings with ideas. Tiny corpses dot the ranch in various stages of decay; if you pick a feather off the ground, it may turn out to have a beak attached. When Eben traps a wood rat, he cuts it open and leaves it near the chicken coop, where it is disemboweled by the hens, who leave only the hide, which becomes part of the soil. The rodent is reincarnated in chicken manure, which goes into compost, which goes onto the garden. Eben's compost gets hot right away — mixed with fresh alfalfa, it sometimes burns up — and he can use it when it's two weeks old. The compost keeps the garden warm even during a frost, so he gardens throughout the winter, stopping only in summer when "it's just too hot and dry."

He uses no pesticides or chemical fertilizers. "I'm agin inorganics. There've been a lot of studies and a lot of people are still living, but I'd rather eat an apple with a worm in it than one from an orchard that got sprayed. I figure if I'm gonna have pesticides on my food, I'll just buy it." He and Gladys buy little. From the ranch they get fruit, vegetables, grains, beans, potatoes, eggs, and beef. The twenty-five or so head of cattle that Eben keeps are "only the number the grass will support." Most local ranchers have to give their livestock hay in winter, but Eben's cattle graze all year long; in summer, when neighboring cows are on the move, searching for grass to eat, Eben's are likely to be lying down, ruminating. He feeds them no hormones or high-protein diets. He seldom has a vet bill.

"The first thing they do to beef when it arrives at the feedlot is spray it, inject it with antibiotics, and implant it with synthetic hormones," Eben says. "The way most cattle are bred now, natural selection isn't working at all. When I was a brand inspector for the state, I'd go to some of these ranches, and down in a creek behind the barn I'd find some kind of throwback creature. For a while there was a bull called the Prince Domino, from the Wyoming Hereford Ranch; everybody had to have Prince Domino the Twenty-seventh or Prince Domino the Thirty-third. It went along okay for about twenty-five years, and then the genetic stability gave out — they started developing dwarfism and cancer eye. The Brahma that came from the agricultural colleges turned out to be tremendously susceptible to sickness and disease. It was a fake, and they had to return to the original bloodline, which goes back five thousand years.

"All of our problems are the result of our intelligence," Eben posits from such evidence. "Out of the houses of higher learning are coming the people who pollute the air and poison the soil. I think the animals that have been most successful in evolution have all been pretty dumb — reptiles, ants, bees. The bee is the epitome of social progress; they've achieved perfect division of labor. If you gave a man a chance in that situation, he'd go in and grab all the honey — or charge all the other bees to get into the hive. When people say animals don't think, I just laugh; animals can adapt to as many situations as humans, but they only do it enough to take care of their needs. I think there's some kind of barrier — a point up to which animals develop in order to be successful in their environment. After they reach it, something happens to shut their sophistication off.

"For me, where man got past that barrier is the million-dollar question. We got along for thousands of years as part and parcel of the environment, but now we're just like pigs at a trough — if you give them enough food for three or four days, they'll fight each other trying to bloat themselves, then keep on fighting after they're full. We're greedy; we're covetous; we hate without knowing what hatred is. Now, if we're to behave like pigs, that's fine as long as we're honest about it; I'm not saying we can necessarily do any different. But I think we should at least close the school doors and stop sending our kids there if this is the best we can do. With all our intelligence and education, we're still doing an awfully poor job of managing something that's been running for millions of years as a very well oiled machine. Man has only been evolving for about one second on the scale of world history, and we haven't even gotten to the middle of the first grade in learning how to get along.

"The typical human being isn't fit for life on this planet," Eben concludes. "If we eliminated waste, the economy would go into a tailspin tomorrow. Nine out of ten men working in industry today are making things that are unnecessary and environmentally destructive. I just read where a computer video company bought four hundred and fifty acres up in Lake County — all rich alluvial land. To produce what? Games about killing, for teenagers to play. Human beings are the prophets of doom. We are the only completely malignant organism in the history of the earth."

ONE OVERCAST MORNING in May, Eben and I got into his truck — a beige '73 Dodge Ranger. Eben was wearing an Atlanta Audubon T-shirt, ankle-high black army boots, green dungarees held up by a pair of red L. L. Bean suspenders (turned inside out so that the red only showed on the trim), and a white boat hat whose wide brim made him look like the Ancient Mariner. If he had undressed for bed the previous night, it wasn't apparent — he'd worn the same clothes the previous day. Nor had he shaved; thick white whiskers covered his face below his heavy sideburns.

We were going to the Carrizo Plain, a singularly dry and remote valley where Eben had worked during the Depression, managing a 60,000-acre ranch. As we got ready, Eben took his garden hose and filled a fire-fighting can with water. "It used to be that, when anybody saw smoke, you'd drop whatever you were doing," he said. "In a year like this with tall grass, a fire could wipe you right out. We'd hit the flames with wet sacks — I've still got about fifty of them in the garage. Nowadays they've got bomber planes to take care of it. My neighbor, he's got a regular little fire truck."

In order to operate the ignition on his truck, Eben reached across the steering column with his left hand. His right hand is deformed, drooping and dilapidated. When he was six years old, he accidentally maimed it with a shotgun and has been unable to grip anything with it since. This doesn't seem to have handicapped him in a life of ranch work; he holds posts with the heel of the hand, uses it as a brace on the handle of a shovel (his left hand serving as a fulcrum and bearing the weight), balances a spoon on top of it when he eats, and shakes hands with his left. To use his rifle, he lays the barrel across the top of the hand and is a crack shot. He was right-handed before the accident.

"It's not hard to learn to use your left hand when you're still a kid," he said, turning onto the county two-lane from the Gillis Canyon Road. "It was just one of those little accidents that usually turn out positive, but this one turned out negative instead. There have been hundreds of times when things happened where I could have been killed, but they turned out positive." As he talked, he was heading into a blind curve in the Palo Prieto Pass road. It's pretty rare to see a car on eastern San Luis Obispo County highways, but suddenly a huge tractor-trailer came roaring around the bend; if the road had had a center stripe, the truck would have been straddling it. Eben whipped the wheel to the right and stomped on the brakes, spewing gravel and hugging a sandstone cliff. The truck vanished as abruptly as it had appeared. Eben pulled back onto the road and said, "That was one of those times right there."

We drove south, into Choice Valley, a landscape characterized by occasional water tanks, solitary cattle, and oceans of yellow grass: oats, barley, clover, filaree. "Looking around here today," Eben said, "you'd probably say ninety-nine percent of the 'native' vegetation was wild oats or foxtail. But there's not a native plant in sight right now. The old government surveyors used to see antelope and elk through here, and the vegetation was always bunch grass. It was here until around 1915 or 1925, and then it just disappeared. As a young fella I saw this happen."

Most of the West's native grasses were wiped out by heavy grazing, and as we drove on, evidence of it was everywhere around us. Some of the hillsides appeared to have been scoured; cattle had stripped the land of its cover, exposing the skin. Eben stopped the truck and pointed at a triangular pasture surrounded by a barbed-wire fence. Inside it were blue-gray atriplex shrubs, buckwheat, blue larkspur, and some tall, stiff grass growing in clumps.

"That's bunch grass," Eben said. "It's been coming back in there since the owner fenced it off — he doesn't have any water to graze livestock. It only survives in an area that's undisturbed, and this plot has been undisturbed for fifteen years. The nude buckwheat there is a native specie. The blue larkspur just got established this year; that's a native shrub. The native perennial grasses are trying to come back all the time."

The former condition of California's rangeland is not a settled issue; some early explorers' reports speak repeatedly of its "barrenness," and some modern agriculturalists opine that the state's original flora was composed mainly of annuals, not perennials. Whatever once existed here, the dominant modern school of thought — one could almost call it a nihilist Darwinism — maintains that the hardiest plants are those that survive, and therefore the present range is the strongest possibility. Eben did not attend this school.

"Before the white man, plants and animals only survived if they had something to offer," he said. "They gave much more than they took. The indigenous plants were the type that would keep animals happy all year round, without encouraging overproduction. They were an advantage to the environment. The exotics are like a cancer — they can only survive in a decaying environment. That's why fertilizer is so necessary — if you offer a drink of whiskey to a tired man, he'll go like the dickens for a short while; but pretty soon he needs more, and after a while he needs a drink every ten steps."

Eben started the truck again and pulled back onto the road. "I've got to get some conservation organizations to subsidize that guy," he said, glancing back at the triangular plot. "I don't think he'd sign an agreement that would restrict him, but maybe, for the amount of the taxes and the water, he'd make a gentleman's agreement to set that plot aside in the public interest until a better opportunity presented itself. I bet twenty-five bucks a year would do it. But you'd have to be careful. Even though he hasn't grazed an animal in there for fifteen years, if you mentioned to him that the native plants were coming back, he might just take it into his head to put a horse in there."

As Eben drove on, he looked at the surrounding grassland and mused: "When the Spaniards first brought cattle to California, it must have been fantastic range country. Just about like the Garden of Eden: no harsh weather, all lush perennial grasses — the cattle must have been fat and slick. It probably lasted forty-five or fifty years. Maybe not even that long, once you get that exponential progression going."

The San Luis Obispo area, like much of the rest of California, was settled in the late 1700s by Spanish missionaries who introduced livestock along with Christianity (as well as most of the state's present plants, whose seeds hitched rides in the hides and tails of the livestock); in 1828, the San Luis Obispo mission had 16,000 head of mature cattle and sheep. The abundant grasslands of which Eben spoke were fenced for the first time after 1835, when the missions were secularized and most of their land was granted to private citizens who had served under the Spanish crown. The ranges were stocked to the limit of their capacity, and by 1862 California contained two million cattle. But the Spanish ranchers, unfamiliar with the region's climatic variations, neglected to store any hay or feed; and ultimately, with the coming of drought between 1862 and 1864, most of the cattle starved.

"They were shooting cattle to save what range there was," said Eben. "They were killing them any way they could — they paid Indians to use bows and arrows on them when they came near the forts. The hide trade was going then; they'd go out, kill the cattle, skin them, and leave the carcass. The condor and grizzly bear populations must have exploded — I bet they reached their highest numbers then."

We passed the tiny, one-room Choice Valley school, which Eben's children had attended when they were growing up. Now empty, it stood by itself in a grove of Chinese elms and California date palms. On the surrounding bare hills with a southern exposure, there was beeweed — low, fuzzy, with blue blossoms. "Cattle won't touch it," Eben said. "It has oil in it. It takes over to cover the earth, just like you would put on a hat. Sometimes, after a drought [Eben pronounced it "drawth"], a lot of the first plants that spring up are poisonous. I don't know if you could use the term wisdom, but nature needs some way to keep the population down for a while. After a number of dry years, the soil will develop selenium, which mows the cattle right down."

Eben pointed at a white flower growing on a hillside. "See that white larkspur growing up there? It's poisonous to cattle. It's an alkaloid — *delphinium* — and it's caused millions of dollars of losses. It comes up around now, when things start getting dry; in combination with the selenium, some years there have been estimated losses of fifty thousand cattle in this country. Cattle can go three or four days without water as long as they have succulents, but at this time of year they'll strip the blossoms right off that larkspur with their lips. You can hear it from a distance. You'll see a herd of cattle start running, and all of a sudden two or three of them'll drop dead. The funny thing is, if it doesn't kill them, they get fat on it."

Eben stopped the truck again, got out, and picked a weed with small, fragile pods hanging from its stalks. *"Astragalus asymmetricus,"* he said. "Locoweed. You should see a horse that's been eating this stuff — he'll be walking along like he's looking at the horizon, and suddenly he stops and shies from something. They get scared of shadows. Locoweed is a hallucinogen. Local cattle seem to know to stay away from it, but cattle from other parts of the country eat it and develop a craving for it. They don't eat anything else, and they get a deficiency."

The pods were about an inch and a half in diameter, hollow and highly crushable. Eben crushed one. Inside, a row of seeds like tiny lima beans sat on a fence of white tendrils. The seeds were slick, almost greasy. "This doctor brought a racehorse down here from Palo Alto once," Eben said. "I told him if he thought much of that horse to take him back up where he came from because we had locoweed around here. He said, Oh, no. In less than three weeks' time, that horse was rearing and shying. Died from lack of water — couldn't find the water trough. Loco horses were very common when I was young. It's a leavening factor. When droughts come along, animals will eat a thing they wouldn't normally eat."

Eben uses certain words in a highly personal way. "Leavening factors" are destructive natural forces — plagues, poisons, predators. ("To leaven bread is to balance or homogenize it," he explains, "the same way nature establishes equality so that no specie has an advantage over any other. Nature has thousands of things up her sleeve just waiting for you to open the gate so they can go to work. The environment is designed to be successful; you might think you're getting the upper hand, but in the long run it'll take you out.") To Eben, anything done with ritual enthusiasm is a "fetish"; good things are "qualitative"; any drug — tobacco, alcohol, marijuana — is a "placebo." ("Something that takes the place of something else," he explained when I asked about that one.) Once, trying to tell me that pain didn't bother him much, Eben said he had a "low threshold" for it. When I asked if he didn't really mean a high threshold, he held his hand in the air over his head. "I think of the pain as being up here," he said. Then he lowered the hand to knee level and said, "No pain is down around here."

In the distance I saw the broad, shimmering, dark green surface of what Eben said was Grant's Lake. When we arrived there, however, the shiny green stuff turned out to be vegetable matter growing in the lakebed, which had only recently dried up. Eben said that Grant's Lake existed only once in a great while, during particularly rainy winters like the one that had just ended. "This is the first succession of plants, to stabilize the soil. When it dies, it'll form a protective blanket. If those plants were palatable to cattle, they wouldn't be there."

"What plants are they?"

"That's a good question. I think I'll just walk down there and take a look."

We got out of the truck and approached the fence that bordered the road. In my experience of barbed-wire etiquette, the party not negotiating the fence holds the wires for the party passing through, but Eben dispensed with this decorum — he held the wires apart for himself, deftly slipped between, and left me to fend for myself. It took me about three times as long to get through the fence as it had taken him (I was worried about ripping my Calvin Klein shirt). When I got to the bottom of the grassy bank, Eben was surveying the shrubs.

"This is pigweed. This is a mallow. This is *Amoranthus.*" Peering closely at the dominant growth in the lakebed, he suddenly exclaimed, "By golly, that's a thistle. No, I don't suppose cattle would eat *that,* would they! In a couple of years this will come back into grass, and it'll be just lush. This is all alluvial material here, like a marsh; if this guy had planted it when it dried up in April, he would've had a tremendous crop. He could have planted corn, barley, watermelons — it would produce three or four times as much as the land up there on the hill. And it would've retained its moisture."

Looking around, Eben observed: "Most of these are introduced plants. I'd like to know what would have grown here after a flood before the white man. I think it might just be this one right here." He was looking at the mallow. "I'm not sure of the specie. I'll have to take some of it with me. I'm gonna find out what that is as soon as I get back."

We renegotiated the fence and got back in the truck. Eben pulled across the highway onto a rutted dirt road and started climbing. Behind the first humps of yellow hill, a wide, steep ditch intersected the road. Eben turned off the engine again and said, "There's a badger down there." I looked through the field glasses toward where he was pointing. Sure enough, a dark, furry creature was ambling away from us. Eben sucked air loudly through his lips. At the squeaking sound, the badger stopped short and looked back toward us. "He might think there's an animal in trouble over here," Eben said, then sucked more air. The badger came running eagerly now. Occasionally it stopped, still staring, but whenever Eben made the sound, the animal galloped toward us again. "The wind's blowing this way, so he won't smell us till he gets right up over the bank," Eben said. Indeed, the badger came all the way up to the edge of the ditch and looked at us through a wall of weeds. Its face was dark, with three light bands running vertically up the bridge of its nose and through its eyes. There were big round ears on top of its head and long, pretty swatches of fur on its legs. The facial stripes made it resemble some sort of wary aborigine, glaring at us for a long moment before it backed down the ditch and disappeared.

"If a quake hit now, half of the truck would go north and the other half would go south," said Eben. "We're right in the fault."

The fault — the ditch — was none other than the San Andreas: boundary of the Pacific and North American continental plates, origin of the 1906 earthquake, specter portending the submersion of America's most populous state. To be sitting on top of this trigger, away from collapsible skyscrapers and freeway overpasses — from anything, in fact, except the badger and the mute yellow hills — felt somehow covert, clandestine; I would say that we were in one of the glamorous fault's low-visibility sectors, but that was literally the opposite of the truth. The border between these continental plates (two of twelve such landmasses in the world) is really more zone than line; it's miles wide in some places and invisible in many (San Francisco, for example). Here it almost looked like the work of a bulldozer; this particular part of the fault thus represented one of its sectors of *highest* visibility.

Eben drove thirty yards farther up the road, turned off the engine again, and began walking stiff-legged downhill toward the ravine. There, alongside the fault where scrub buckwheat was growing, was what appeared to be a corrugated steel garbage can that someone had buried up to the lid. Eben bent over, grabbed the handle, and removed the lid. Inside were several wet-cell batteries and a meter with one end of a high-tensile wire connected to it. The wire disappeared into a conduit on one side of the can. Eben said that the meter was recording movement along the fault — it belonged to the United States Geological Survey, based in Menlo Park.

"Right now somebody up there's probably charting our footsteps," Eben surmised. Actually, nobody was. The device we were looking at, I later learned, was a "creepmeter." It was intended, as Eben said, to measure movement along the fault, but all it was able to record was the gradual shifting of continental plates in relation to each other, and it's doubtful that our presence (however weighty) could affect that.

The San Andreas is only one of many thousands of earthquake faults in California, but it is by far the biggest — 650 miles long and 20 miles deep — and it has been the source of two of the three major earthquakes that have occurred in the state's short recorded history. (The most famous one, of course, was San Francisco's, in 1906. The other big San Andreas quake happened in 1857 along the southern part of the fault; strongest in the vicinity of Fort Tejon, it threw the Los Angeles River out of its bed and reversed the flow of the Ventura. A third quake that would have measured eight on the Richter scale — estimated from descriptions of its effects, since there wasn't any Richter scale in 1872 — occurred in the Owens Valley, on the eastern side of the Sierra Nevada.) This distinction, along with its proximity to two of the largest population centers in the United States, has now made the San Andreas the single most *studied* earthquake fault in the world: between the cities of Hayward (which has another fault named after it east of San Francisco but is still part of the San Andreas "zone") in the north and Palmdale in the south, the USGS has thirty-two creepmeters, eight tiltmeters, four strainmeters, seventeen dilatometers, ten water-level recorders, twenty-three magnetometers, and two hundred seismometers. Oddly, this army of instruments is only theoretically useful in the prediction of earthquakes. It has been in existence for just about twenty years, so the USGS has no previous big-quake experience to relate to the mass of data it's collecting; it will only be able to interpret "premonitory" signals after the next big quake occurs.

I learned all this from a technician named Sandra Schultz at the USGS's Menlo Park headquarters when I went there later to uncover the purpose of the meter Eben had shown me. I found out that it was Schultz's baby; she drives down to check on the device every month, charting creep in the fault. A slight woman with a soft voice, Schultz told me in no uncertain terms that she was "dedicated to creep."

Creep is not a common phenomenon. The only other places it is being studied are Ismet Pasa, Turkey, and Xi'an, China, which have right-lateral slip faults similar to the San Andreas. If you stand on either side of such a fault and look across, the opposite side is slipping to your right: creeping. This movement, where it occurs, is going on all the time; but it isn't taking place over the entire length of the San Andreas — only from San Juan Bautista (the southern limit of the repercussions from the 1906 quake) to the place where Eben and I stood, 135 miles to the south. The point where the creep is greatest — about 28 millimeters per year — is halfway in between, near King City. North of San Juan Bautista and south of Palo Prieto Pass, the fault is locked — that is, not moving at all. Schultz said that there are conflicting theories on the meaning of this. Some geologists think that creep releases strain in the fault and thus reduces the likelihood of a big quake. Others believe that creep is an *indication* of strain; they theorize that the far northern and southern sections of the San Andreas used to creep before they had their earthquakes, and that the midsection, which is creeping now, is therefore due for the next Big One — an event that might start San Francisco and Fort Tejon creeping again.

A good place to see the effects of creep is the town of Hollister, "the earthquake capital of the world," about 50 miles south of San Jose. Built on top of a crazy quilt of earthquake faults and traces, Hollister experiences something on the order of a hundred microquakes a day. Northwest of town, three faults — the Busch, the Sargent, and the Calaveras — form a triangle; to the south, the Calaveras intersects the San Andreas. On its way to do so, it cuts through the middle of town. Like the San Andreas, the Calaveras is a right-lateral slip fault, and in some parts of Hollister, its creep has resulted in broken curbstones, curved concrete retaining walls, and sidewalks that bend to no pedestrian purpose. The scarp of the fault has terraced the otherwise level lawn of a park. A block away, telephone poles tilt at crazy angles beside a house whose convex walls lean away from the street; the fault runs right underneath the house, half of which is heading toward Mexico. The other half is bound for Alaska; from an upstairs window, you can almost make out the Aleutians coming over the horizon.

The last quake of any magnitude (5.0) to strike near Eben's house occurred in 1966. It didn't do much damage aside from downing power lines and toppling groceries from supermarket shelves. Eben said he knew somebody who claimed to have been watching the fault at the time: "He said it was opening and closing like an accordion. Every time there was a bump, a cloud of dust went up. From the kind of guy he was, I'd trust his integrity on it." The earthquake offset the yellow line in Highway 46 by four inches, which increased to eight as creep continued for two weeks. In May of

1983, a 6.2 quake on the Nuñez Fault, centered at Coalinga — 30 miles north of Cholame — actually reversed the direction of creep in the nearby section of the San Andreas, which, for about a year afterward, became a left-lateral slip fault. (Now that part of the fault has begun creeping to the right again.)

The winter preceding the Coalinga quake had been quite wet, and some people think the shift was brought on by draining groundwater as the earth dried out. Eben voiced another theory: "The first reports that came out, several geologists indicated there was information that would implicate the removal of oil. There was a situation like that in Colorado — earthquakes were happening until they stopped pumping out oil, and then the earthquakes stopped. That there around Coalinga is one of the oldest oil fields in the state. The quake was pretty near limited to that oil basin. Now they're saying it's a thirty-thousand-foot-deep fault that they never knew was there before. If there's any evidence that would incriminate human activity, they'll just squelch it. California's so conscious of bringing in industry and tourism — in Los Angeles now it's against the law to say on anybody's death certificate that they died from smog. You have to say emphysema or lung cancer, even if their lungs are black. In California there's a lot of that. It's getting so that official information is completely unreliable."

We got back in the truck and crossed the fault again, descending through the hills to the highway. A flock of birds went by. "Look at those starlings tearing along!" Eben exclaimed. "Let's catch them and see how fast they're going." He gunned the engine and took out after the flock like a highway patrolman. Ahead, the birds were rising and falling in columns as they raced down the highway, a spirited profusion of black dots against the drabness of the day. Watching through the windshield, I felt as if I were in a George

Lucas movie, chasing a shower of asteroids across some gray and yellow planet. "They must be going fifty," Eben said, watching his speedometer. "I found out that the average speed of birds in the air is between thirty-six and thirty-eight miles an hour. The funny thing is, the fastest birds are the ones you don't expect. You wouldn't think robins were that fast, but they get up pretty near fifty. Hawks are only fast when they dive, because of gravity. An ordinary old pigeon will fly right away from a falcon going up a canyon, but falcons and eagles reach two hundred miles an hour on the dive. I've seen eagles dive and a quarter of a mile away the air would roar just like an airplane."

I was reminded of a story a friend had told me, so I related it to Eben. This friend has a big yard — half an acre, a veritable farm by Oakland standards — where doves like to roost. One day, when he was in the yard, a flock of doves took off from the power lines all at once. Suddenly a small raptor — a falcon, my friend thought — plunged into the middle of the flock, nabbing one dove and bringing it to earth. The falcon was mantling — spreading its wings over — the dove when my friend noticed the family cat creeping toward both birds through the bushes. Though not a little concerned for his cat, my friend was so transfixed by the mounting drama that he couldn't bring himself to intervene. The cat pounced; the falcon took off; the dove — none the worse for wear, apparently, despite having played meal ticket to two predators in the space of sixty seconds — got away.

"I'll be danged!" Eben exclaimed before telling me that the "falcon" was in all likelihood a sharp-shinned hawk. "Falcons kill their prey in the air. They swipe it behind the head with their talons, then go back and pick it up. The sharp-shinned hawk is an accipiter — they're short-winged, long-tailed, quick. They can attack through the trees. I saw one catch a quail once and pluck almost all its feathers off.

The quail's eyes were blinking the whole time. When I walked up, the hawk took off and the quail ran away."

We rounded a bend and, as if to footnote our discussion, a redtailed hawk rose suddenly from the shoulder of the road, carrying a snake. It looked like a helicopter trailing a rope ladder. The hawk came to earth in a brown furrowed field about a hundred yards away. Eben handed me the binoculars so that I could inspect the hawk's stern, magisterial countenance, seemingly aloof to the thrashing of the snake under its talons.

"I bet if we go up there he'll abandon the snake, but come back for it when we leave," Eben said. We got out and approached the bird, which took off — without the snake — and perched on a distant telephone pole. When we reached the still-squirming snake, it turned out to be headless; there was a bloody nub instead of a skull, which was probably on top of the telephone pole, in the hawk. Eben picked up the twisting ex-reptile, a gopher snake.

"They're pretty well camouflaged when they're on their belly," he said. "I'll take him back down to the pavement and turn him over. If we put him in the middle of the road, the hawk will have a chance to see him and cars won't run him over." When we drove away, the hawk was still on the telephone pole. "Here comes a raven," Eben said. "When the hawk sees him he'll go get the snake; if he doesn't, the raven will. That's too much protein to go to waste."

Within a few miles, we came out onto a broad tableland. Far in the distance I could see the craggy violet outline of the La Panza Mountains. We were now approaching the region of the San Juan Ranch, where Eben had worked for fifteen years. The ranch was originally owned by Henry Wreden, a San Francisco brewer who ran something called the Pinole Land and Cattle Company from it. Eben signed on in 1937, "at the rock bottom of the Depression. I'd go into the Department of Labor office in Bakersfield looking for men. They'd come out on freight trains and were all grimy, but, boy, they were sitting there waiting to spring. Then, after two weeks, when they got their first paycheck, they'd get pretty independent — they weren't so sure if they wanted to work or not."

When Wreden died toward the end of the Depression, the land was divided among six of his heirs. Eben agreed to stay on as an adviser to one of them, William P. Wreden, a rare book dealer in Palo Alto. The San Juan Ranch had always been used for grazing, but after it was split up Eben convinced Bill Wreden that the land should be farmed in wheat. They burned off the grass, plowed the land, and planted it in November. That winter the region received twice its average rainfall; falling upon wheat planted in virgin soil, it enabled Wreden to realize a profit of 80,000 Depression-era dollars. Eben's share was around $7,000, and he used it to buy his own ranch. But now, as we approached the area and Eben reflected on his decision to farm it, he said, "Maybe I shouldn't have. In the long run it would've been better for the land if I hadn't. As manager of a ranch, my job was dependent on production — I had to go for the highest yield possible. I thought I was doing something great and progressive, but I was ignorant of environmental responsibility. I broke up that sod, which had been there since time immemorial, without any knowledge of the chain of events that would follow. That soil was black at first; now it's light. You used to be able to drive through there for miles; now there are big chasms from erosion. It's washed away and blown away. From a pristine, fruitful land, it's degenerated down to nothing."

It wasn't logical for Eben to take personal responsibility for this; sooner or later, it seemed to me, someone would have plowed the San Juan Ranch. But Eben said, "I would a whole lot rather look back at my past as being part of a social movement that provided enough for everybody, with the land coming first." He gazed at the scene before us: spacious skies, amber waves of grain, majestic purple mountains above a fruited plain. "I feel guilty," he said.

On rainfall maps of California, all of the areas that we think of as desert are in the southeastern part of the state, save one: a dry little pocket halfway between Bakersfield and San Luis Obispo that gets about five inches of precipitation annually. This is the Carrizo Plain, which derives its extreme aridity from its situation in the rainshadow of several sets of mountains. To the immediate west are the La Panzas and Calientes, part of the rainmongering topographical network referred to as the California Coast Ranges. To the east are the Temblors, a barren-looking spur of 4,000-foot-high hills, which get even less rain than the Carrizo (about four inches a year) and are the only thing separating it from the dessicated oil country in the southern part of the San Joaquin Valley. The San Andreas Fault runs straight down the Carrizo side of the Temblors, which, in combination with the land's nakedness, makes this area literally the best place in the world to see streambeds offset by seismic activity: the drainages on the Temblors' western flank all take doglegs to the right (as in right-lateral slip) as soon as they hit the fault. Once upon a time, water flowing down these slopes may have continued north into the Salinas River or south into the Cuyama, but the present Carrizo Plain (elevation: 2,000 feet) has no drainage outlet whatsoever — perhaps a result of earthquake upheavals in the past. What little rain falls here in winter stays, forming Soda Lake, so named because of the layer of sodium phosphate that's left behind when the lake dries up in summer. These white alkaline deposits provide a protective visual backdrop for sandhill cranes, which use the Carrizo as a wintering spot; the broad, flat valley floor — 10 miles wide, on average; 40 from north to south — is historically a favorite foraging ground for condors, which left their roosts in the nearby mountains to feed on carcasses of the deer, elk, and antelope that originally populated the plain. The salinity of the area surrounding Soda Lake was, in general, unattractive to farmers; the Spanish land grants were all to the west and north, and the roads that developed between Los Angeles and San Francisco followed them. As a result, the Carrizo Plain, for all its uniqueness, remains one of California's least-known niches.

This obscurity was the target of a clever attack during the 1960s, when a group of real estate investors created something called California Valley just north of Soda Lake. They subdivided an 18,000-acre ranch and bulldozed a grid of access roads, complete with corner street signs, claiming that any place equidistant from Los Angeles and San Francisco and "halfway from the Sierra to the sea" would be "a strategic spot to stake your future in land." The actual isolation of the site did not dissuade them. In May of 1963, they threw a barbecue for 23,000 prospective homebuyers. They established a bimonthly newsletter, the *Valley Herald,* publicizing the project's latest developments — the installation of fire service, the building of a swimming pool, recent visits by various owners — and an advice column called "Sam Rawhide Sez" ("Come when you can. Enjoy your land"). Advertisements for this amazingly unprolific area proclaimed that it was "growing people." However, a lack of electrical power and the poor quality of the water that was supposed to irrigate the people blocked that scheme from fruition. Since 1971, California Valley has grown exactly fifty-one registered voters; seven thousand two-and-a-half-acre "ranchos" have failed to grow any houses. The nearest high school remains 50 miles away. Still standing are several structures intended to facilitate the following of Sam Rawhide's advice: a motel, an airstrip, a restaurant, a service station, and a community center into which Eben and I now pulled so that I could use the bathroom. When I came out, Eben was leaning forward with his elbows on a fence, staring at the ground. "Here's a highly successional plant," he said.

In the packed earth beside the parking lot, tiny herbs — the kind you buy in health food stores — were sprouting. "Chamomile," Eben said. "You'd never find that out in the grass, away from this dirt. Look at those poppies — they'll only grow in weak soil where there's no competition." Looking around the parking lot, Eben said, "Horticulture people have no sense of values. Why is it that almost all the trees planted here are exotic? We have natives that'll grow just as good — maybe better. Here's a native plant trying to grow right here." He was pointing to a plant with a spiral shape and furry edges. "Squirrel plant. If you give the natives half a chance . . ."

Getting back into the truck, Eben said, "This has been a poor year for wildflowers and successional plants. They come in the first year after an area has been ruined — burned or something. But this is our fifth year in a row of above-average rainfall. That's a most unusual situation for vegetation. It might be the first time we've ever had that many years of rain back-to-back. Usually you'll have wet, moderate, drought . . . back and forth."

The wealth of rain was responsible for the continuing presence of Soda Lake, which came into view on our left as we began to drive south. "Usually it's dry by this time," said Eben, eyeing the flat blue and white expanse. Stretching before us in the middle distance was the Carrizo Plain itself, an undifferentiated scrubland to my untrained eye, but on closer inspection — Eben's habit — a complicated community of plants. Alongside the road was a band of green fescue with delicate, translucent tops waving in the wind. Beyond that, grassy bromes predominated, providing a base that was punctuated at intervals by dull blue-green *atriplex* shrubs, clusters of yellow goldfield flowers, and purple larkspur standing slender amid the brown-green brome.

"There probably used to be some relationship between the atriplex and the antelope and tule elk," Eben said. "When I was a kid, I knew an old-timer who remembered the original alluvial floodplains; he said they were full of atriplex, and everywhere they had that there was antelope. In those days the Carrisa would have had less of the things that are common here now — less jackrabbits, less squirrels. More grizzly bears. There's a record of a grizzly grazing on the Cholame Flat. Probably the densest population of grizzlies in the state was in the Los Osos Valley, near San Luis Obispo. The Spaniards used to catch them and put them in a pen with a bull and make bets on the winner."*

Carrisa — Eben's word for Carrizo — is the accepted local usage, appearing in such official venues as newspapers and on road signs.† The Spanish word *carrizo* referred to a cane-like reed grass that grew to be ten feet tall; the Indians made sugar from its sap and traded it to the Spaniards. Eben said he had some seeds for the stuff and was considering planting them in the Carrizo Plain "just so they'd have some of their namesake grass." Such a move would actually constitute an

---

* According to *Duhaut-Cilly's Account of California in the Years 1827–28,* "The beginning of this mortal struggle was always in the bull's favor; but when some deep bite or the fatigue from the combat forced him to thrust out his tongue, the bear never failed to seize him by this sensitive part, and to bury his terrible claws into it; not letting go his hold, whatever struggles his adversary made. The bull, conquered, reduced to bellowing frightfully, torn in every part, fell exhausted and bled to death."

† This etymological adjustment is in keeping with what the novelist Thomas McGuane has called "the great Western tradition of corrupting language into the grunting of the midland yokel who levels the same Mortimer Snerd suspicion upon all human products, but starts with language." McGuane offers the example of the *mecate*, a rope developed by Spanish horsemen, which modern American cowboys refer to as the "McCarthy."

exotic introduction; the bastardization of the original term is somewhat appropriate, as carrizo grass has never grown on the Carrizo Plain. The predominant cover as we got farther south was the ubiquitous, pestiferous, insidious ingredient of the California landscape: *Hordeum jubatum* — foxtail barley.

The luxuriant hills of the Golden State, so inviting at a distance, are coated with this infernal growth, which derives its nickname from the resemblance of its blades to the posterior part of a native animal noted for being clever. In spring, *Hordeum jubatum* bestows a moist and undulant verdure; come summer, however, the blades dry out, and then the analogy with the supple foxtail is more honestly drawn with an arrowhead. Ever since I came to California, I have been wanting to get this off my chest about foxtail grass: *It gets in your clothes and it won't come out and it sticks you.* The only way to remove the blades is to turn your clothes inside out, buy a magnifying glass, use it to locate the tiny barb, affix the nails of your thumb and index finger to the point, and pull it through in the same direction in which it started. *Hordeum jubatum* thus operates on an adherence principle identical to that of the porcupine quill; the difference between foxtail barley and a porcupine is that, in the case of the porcupine, one easily recognizes the advantage of being obnoxious. (In this I admit to a common prejudice favoring vertebrate animals; I once challenged Eben to give me some evolutionary rationale for the irritating efficiency of foxtail, and after he replied the answer seemed obvious. By clinging to all manner of mobile creatures, the plant has achieved distribution over so wide and varied a range that no single adverse environmental development could ever wipe it out.)

We passed a herd of sheep now, dull brown and dust-covered, looking altogether uncomfortable in the beating midday heat. "Look at all those sheep!" Eben exclaimed. "Boy, you'd think their coats would just be foxtail and nothing else! Wouldn't that be a miserable life? To be a sheep in fox-tail country?" As if to underscore the point, there appeared in the road ahead a lone, disoriented ewe; the sheep looked like some kind of postnuclear survivor — stunned, bleeding, emaciated. It gave no appearance of knowing where it was, or caring.

"I bet dogs got on him," Eben said. "I don't think he's gonna be good for much. It's irresponsible to let something like that live. You ought to kill a sheep like that if you're going to be killing coyotes — it's just an invitation to them."

After another minute of slow driving, we made out a body lying in the shimmering heat of the road ahead. Another fig-ure was standing next to it. As we approached, the upright figure — a man with dark skin — moved to the side of the road; the prone torso got up and put its hands on its hips. When we got closer, we could see that it was a boy about ten years old. He was wearing a red baseball cap with white polka dots and a gray baseball shirt with yellow sleeves. He waited until we were right beside him, then brazenly stuck out his thumb as if asking for a ride.

Eben slowed to a stop and announced, "I want to buy fif-teen sheep."

The boy raised himself up on his toes, looked into the back of the truck, then looked back at Eben and said, "Where's you gonna put 'em?"

Eben stared through the windshield, thinking. "In our stomachs," he said. "We're gonna have a sheep barbecue up at Painted Rocks."

"You got any sodas?" the boy asked. "I'll buy one from you."

"No," said Eben. Then, gesturing toward the dark-skinned man: "You helping him herd sheep?"

The boy said, "I'm teachin' him how."

"How do you know how?"

"Learned it all my life." He shrugged.

"Is he Peruvian?"

The boy spit in the dirt and nodded.

Eben said, "They've got an animal down there called a vicuña. Call him over here."

The boy waved to the dark-skinned man, who approached the truck.

Eben said, "¿Perú? ¿Sabe vicuña?"

The man shook his head. "Soy de Jalisco. En México. ¿Perú?"

"You know," said Eben, "there's a sheep back up the road who looks like he got run over."

"Oh yeah," the boy said. "I know him. We tied him up for bait. Coyotes tore him up. I got five of 'em with my seven-millimeter." He raised his arms, one extended away from him, the other alongside his face, and squeezed twice with his index finger. "Spic-boom! Spic-boom!"

"Well," Eben remarked, "when they're tough out on the Carrisa Plains, they're *real* tough, aren't they?"

"That's what you get when you been in fourteen fights. Guy at school hit me with a baseball bat last week. You know how Mexicans fight. I don't fool around with 'em — I just gave him a couple of one-two-threes." The boy leaned away and spit again.

"You got snoose?" Eben asked.

"Uh-huh."

"Think I could have a pinch?"

The boy pulled a tin of Skoal from his back pocket and handed it to Eben. Eben took a pinch and handed it back. Before the boy put it in his pocket, he took some more himself.

"By golly, look at that!" exclaimed Eben. "If I took that much, they'd be patting me in the face with a shovel! I'm about half-dizzy right now."

As we drove away, leaving the boy and man alone in the

middle of the desert, Eben said, "If you ran into one of these kids out here forty years ago, he would have been bashful, looking down at the ground. Not anymore, boy. They've got *Star Wars*. He was just as nonchalant — no sense of inferiority a'tall. I'd like to've been hiding somewhere and heard his conversation with that Mexican."

More of the omnipresent khaki sheep crossed the road, bleating as they went. Watching them pass, Eben moaned, "Where you from? *Mon-taaaaana.* Where you going? *Baaaaack.*"

Soon we departed from the flat dirt road that constitutes the Carrizo's principal thoroughfare. Across the plain, an enormous mass of rock loomed up like an island; we beat toward it through a sea of barley, bucking the wave of a rutted ranch track. Eben was flabbergasted by the rippling grain, which was almost as tall as we were ("Boy, what a great crop! This is really something!"). As we approached the giant rocks, we began to discern groups of darting specks peeling into the sky in sheets and then, by turns, returning to the rocks. Cliff swallows: a convention of them in the middle of the prairie, filling the air, fluttering, chirping, hovering, racing, poking their heads from the holes in their mud nests, hundreds of which were affixed to the cliff face and to each other like the nests of wasps.

"An oriole's nest is standardized," said Eben, "but each of these has to be modified according to the shape of the one next to it. The swallow family is a good example of divergent evolution. Bank swallows are similar to these, but they dig their holes in banks. The rough-winged swallow also digs holes, but only lives in pairs. Groups of birds branch off and develop different characteristics to utilize some part of the environment that the parent specie doesn't. When they built I-5, cliff swallows increased by the thousands — they nest under the overpasses."

The birds had black backs and heads, reddish-brown

throats, white bellies, and white foreheads that shone from the nests like spotlights. "A good example of adaptive coloring," said Eben. "If it weren't for that white forehead, another swallow flying by wouldn't be able to tell if any bird was inside the nest. It's like a signpost that says 'occupied.' It's not important for swallows not to be seen; it's important for them to *be* seen. Now, this is just my own theory; I might be wrong."

"Why do they keep taking off and coming back?"

"It's a practice run. In nature as in human beings, in order to be proficient you have to be experienced; if those swallows just waited there for some predator to be on the wing and away, they wouldn't have a chance. It's a defensive reaction. Some message must have come to that group that just took off."

"From that redtailed hawk, maybe?"

"No. The redtail and the swallow have a symbiotic relationship — the redtail protects the swallow against accipitors and other predators. There are other examples of that in this country; the ground squirrel and the burrowing owl live together in pretty good style. You'll even find rattlesnakes in the same hole with burrowing owls."

We continued on to another set of rocks that towered some 200 feet above the plain, full of caves, chambers, and hollows. The rocks, big as they were, almost appeared to have been arranged in a circle; in the middle of this gargantuan "boulder" a couple of hundred feet in diameter was a kind of grassy amphitheater, its eastern end open, looking across the flat Carrizo toward the multiridged, milk chocolate Temblors. We left the truck and walked inside. There on the orange and yellow lichen-covered walls of rock were ancient anthropomorphic figures, intricately painted in red, black, and white — worn and weathered pictographs of the long-vanished Chumash Indians.

A romantic man named Myron Angel, in a book entitled

The Painted Rock of California (which he published himself in
1910), had this to say about the rock where Eben and I now
stood:

> Most awe-inspiring and mysterious, and most indubitably
> the work of the Sun-worshipers, are the Sphinx of Egypt
> and the Painted Rock of San Luis Obispo, standing almost
> precisely opposite each other on the globe. . . . the latter is
> known to but few, though its existence as a temple may be
> of equal age and its purpose the same, both facing the rising
> sun, and both great and mysterious works of an unknown
> people. . . . aborigines and the early Mexican ranchero re-
> vered the rock and its paintings as something sacred, but
> the iconoclastic Anglo-Saxon has little reverence for any-
> thing, and thus the curious hunters, to the shameful dis-
> honor of civilization, have mutilated them. . . . A pleasant
> and healthful climate over all made this an ideal home for a
> large number of peaceful aborigines of the country. . . . the
> supply of food appears to have been so abundant that there
> was no struggle for existence, and the climate so even and
> delightful that they showed their appreciation of these
> conditions by crowding it with a dense population, which,
> for a long period, enjoyed a peaceful and indolent life.
> Excavations into the cemeteries show that many of the
> localities had been occupied continuously, probably FOR
> TEN CENTURIES AT LEAST. . . . Here, in a structure
> created by the Great Architect of the Universe, these people
> of this western wilderness had created a temple rivalling
> the greatest temples of the world and standing at this time
> as one of the most sacred and lasting monuments of man-
> kind.

Mr. Angel, it probably need not be pointed out, was given
to hyperbole. Even if the Chumash had arranged the
Painted Rocks in a circle — which is doubtful unless they
had access to some stimulant that has since been eradicated

by overgrazing (in which case cattle would now rule California) — Egypt and the Carrizo Plain do not stand opposite each other on the globe. And as to the "dense population" of natives, while the Chumash did have seasonal villages in the area, in general they found it no more hospitable than did the Europeans who eventually annihilated them, and stuck to the coast.

California Indians have never enjoyed a lofty reputation; in a syndrome that continues to characterize outside attitudes toward inhabitants of the state, their civilization is viewed as deficient because of a coddling climate. Even the latter-day revisionist Richard Brautigan pointed out, in *A Confederate General from Big Sur*, that California's coastal people "didn't wear any clothes. They didn't have any fire or shelter or culture. They didn't grow anything. They didn't hunt and they didn't fish. They didn't bury their dead or give birth to their children. They lived on roots and limpets and sat pleasantly out in the rain." The Chumash, however (who may have been the state's first urbanites; early European explorers found several villages that contained populations of a thousand or more), were regarded by the Spanish as superior to the other "peaceful and indolent" California tribes they encountered. They were called intelligent, inventive, and amiable — Gaspar de Portolá's men reportedly never "met natives so affectionate." Besides being known for their paintings, they were noted for making fine wooden plates and bowls, geometrically woven baskets, and a fast, frameless, seagoing canoe of which Father Antonio de la Ascension wrote in 1602: "Since Noah's ark a finer and lighter vessel with timbers better made has not been seen." Alas, an ark was in order. In a familiar, tragic scenario, once the admiring Caucasians intermingled with the Chumash, syphilis, smallpox, pleurisy, pneumonia, infanticide, and abortion spread quickly among the natives; an epidemic in

1801 nearly wiped them out. Eventually they revolted against Spanish rule, for which they were further punished and exterminated. Today it is impossible to find a full-blooded Chumash Indian; all that remains are their pictographs, which have never been granted protection by the state and which, as a result, have been all but destroyed by the Anglo-Saxons, whom the otherwise unreliable Angel characterized with accuracy.

"You have to wonder what in the human spirit would do such a thing," Eben said, staring at a painting accompanied by the signature of Dilbert S. Ninas, 1956. "You can see here where people have shot at them; here W. J. Hamilton chipped the paint off to put his name. When I first came here it was just vivid — there was a centipede sort of form the whole length of this rock. If in 1925 this had been preserved, it would still be nice. But in those days, the only good Indian was still a dead Indian. The thought of preserving things was so far beyond anybody's comprehension . . ."

Standing before the eroded images, I was pointedly reminded of the ephemeral nature of art: that it is, after all, mere surface decoration. Where the pigment had been scraped away, the timeless rock reasserted itself and the work of human imagination seemed feeble. Yet even in this degraded, indistinct form, the images offered the privilege of history more directly than any protected painting, framed and lit on the wall of a museum. Art encountered in its aboriginal setting, unfenced and unadvertised, rockets you back through time and preconception until you stand alongside the creator of the thing, surrounded by bunch grass and antelope and grizzly, in a land you can never truly lay claim to but love in the manner of an adopted child, pretending to be in the bosom of your real family.

Back on the road, we ran into an out-of-gas cowboy in a beige Dodge pickup identical to ours. Eben stopped to offer assistance and engage the fuelless horseman in conversation. At first the cowboy was extremely taciturn, but after we'd given him some gas through a siphon (an "Oklahoma credit card," according to Eben), he invited us back to the ranch where he worked in order to reimburse us. In passing, Eben asked if the ranch was a sheep outfit; the cowboy gave a derisive laugh and shook his head as if we had to be kidding. Eben declined the offer of payment, saying that we were botanists and had to get on with our trip.

"Just so he'd know we weren't itinerants wandering around," Eben said after the cowboy had departed. "I tell him we're botanists in defense, the same way he wanted us to know that he wasn't a sheepman. 'No!' he says, just like I'd asked him, 'Are you some kind of a freak?' It's interesting to see that the old antagonism is still there between the sheepmen and the cowmen—from the old, historic days. Did you see how, when we first pulled up, he was acting kind of unsociable? That's the way — to keep some kind of distance or dignity. He warmed up once he saw we were helpful. Probably, if we'd taken him up on that offer to reimburse us for the gas, he would've shown us his saddle or something — just to prove he was a rugged cowperson and a friendly guy."

Off to the right was a lone hillock — not a rock, like Painted Rock, but a rocky hill. Eben parked on the side of the road and we walked across the prairie toward "Coyote Hill." As we started making our way up the boulders, Eben said, "Anywhere you have a rocky hill there'll be rattlesnakes," and within sixty seconds we heard the notorious, high-pitched vibration that probably resides in the collective unconscious — a baby rattler, decorated with brown and yellow bands that matched the tones of the surrounding countryside, was coiled between two rocks. Eben waved the toe of his boot past the snake's nose, and the reptile recoiled instantly, like a rubberband: a well-engineered, high-tech animal. "I think you could put your finger down there within two inches of that snake and it wouldn't strike," said Eben. "They depend on their protective coloration. If it wasn't this way, you'd have ten cattle killed every day."

On top of the hill, we looked out over the broad Carrizo. Writing about the "Carrisa Plains" in *Man and the California Condor,* Eben's brother Ian noted that "panoramic variety marked the general region as condor country," and it was certainly in evidence now. Behind us, backlit by the lowering sun, were the craggy Calientes, where Eben and Ian made their first forays into condor nests as boys. To the north was infinite flatness, with the silver ribbon of Soda Lake discernible in the distance. Far to the south, barely visible in the blue haze like a Californian Kilimanjaro, was the white snow peak of Mount Pinos, today's premiere condor-watching destination. The view to the east was cut off by the Temblors, whose ridges and folds and fault-altered streambeds were accentuated by the long afternoon light. Everywhere else, as far as I could see, were red, brown, and yellow grasses with green patches distributed evenly among them. Eben said that the green spots were "Neema mounds" built by kangaroo rats, animals he described as "agents of man's rehabilitation."

"They move into depleted lands and build up weak soil by packing grass into their burrows," he said. "When they clear it out in the spring, you can see it's very rich organic matter; that's why there's tall green grass growing over their mounds. Up until around 1830, the kangaroo rat was evolving along with perennial grass; the grasses on these mounds now have only come along in the last hundred and fifty years. They tend to work against the kangaroo rat, which is a burrowing animal; if you put it in eight-inch grass, it's in a lot of trouble — it can't negotiate. The kangaroo rat might not be able to compete with exotic plants. I'm not giving the specie too many years before it's extinct."

When we got back to the truck, we turned toward the Temblors, following another dirt spur off the main road. "I don't want to drive across that grass," Eben explained. "It's so dry, and as botanists we're the last people who can afford to start a range fire." We began ascending through a brown, grassy, rugged canyon dotted with small green pines — *Ephedra viridus,* "sheepherder's tea." The opposing slopes of the canyon resembled each other only in their steepness; their vegetation was completely different. The north-facing hillsides were (relatively) lush, with bright green goldenbush and yellow *Coreopsis* among the brome. The much drier southern exposures were painted with a subtler palette: dull blue atriplex, spiky green yucca, red brome, tan foxtail, and flesh-colored exposed sand. The clear line of demarcation was the hard white road on which we traveled at the bottom of the canyon, following a dry streambed.

We came to a cattle gate and Eben got out. "If we ran into a locked gate here, we'd be justified in forcing our way through," he said. "This is all BLM land — public domain. Here on this land ranchers get their roads maintained, their fences repaired, their stock watered, and their predators controlled — and it costs them half as much to graze livestock for a month as it does private landowners. Then a lot of them lock the gates in places like this, where they really have no right."

The BLM — Bureau of Land Management — administers about 15 percent of the land in the United States. Much of it is rented to ranchers for a grazing fee that fluctuates with livestock prices and ranchers' operating costs but is always much cheaper than the cost of leasing private grazing land. In 1981, federal agencies collected $24.9 million in such fees, but after sharing the revenues with local governments and paying $58.5 million to manage the grasslands, the U.S. Treasury was left with a deficit of $33.6 million — a subsidy to the ranchers, essentially, footed by the nation's taxpayers. In Oregon that year, this subsidy amounted to more than $2,000 for every rancher using BLM land — two years after the agency admitted that 135 million of the 170 million acres of western rangeland it managed were in "fair" condition or worse, primarily because of overgrazing.

The BLM began life as the U.S. Grazing Service, formed as a consequence of the Taylor Grazing Act in 1934. The aim of the service and the act was to correct the overgrazing and soil deterioration that had begun with the boisterous westward expansion that followed the Civil War. Thousands of nomadic herders were prohibited from grazing by the Taylor Act, which disqualified those owning an insufficient amount of land or livestock. But the original settlers' optimism about the West's unlimited resources was passed on to their progeny, who by the early 1940s had begun lobbying congressmen to keep the grazing fees low and maintain a lot of livestock on public lands. In 1947 Congress went so far as to cut the Grazing Service appropriations in half and reduce its personnel by two thirds, leaving one worker to enforce regulations for every three million acres. A bill was introduced in the Senate to sell off BLM lands, national forest grazing land, and even parts of national parks at low prices with minuscle rates of interest; it was staved off by conservationists, including the western historian Bernard DeVoto, whose *Harper's* articles aroused the public. Meanwhile the grazing permits, which carried so many advantages, acquired a market value of their own; today they are accepted as security for bank loans, included in the appraised value of property, and bought and sold along with ranches and livestock, sometimes bringing prices approaching a thousand dollars per animal. Ranchers who have paid that kind of money for their permits don't cotton to federally mandated reductions in the number of animals they may graze — a syndrome that has played havoc with the condition of public lands.

In 1974, a BLM study concluded that livestock on public ranges in Nevada had laid waste to that state's wildlife, watersheds, and recreation. A federal court subsequently ordered the BLM to produce site-specific environmental impact statements analyzing the effects of grazing; Congress then passed the Federal Land Policy and Management Act, requiring the BLM to involve the public, to sustain a variety of uses on its lands, and to retain them in federal ownership. The result was a resolution in the Nevada state legislature that maintained that federal land within the state's borders rightfully belonged to the state; it said that the U.S. Government ought to relinquish its claim to this property so that the state could sell it. Similar resolutions arose in the legislatures of several western states, touching off the so-called Sagebrush Rebellion, which only later lost steam when the ranchers realized that foreigners (A-rabs and their ilk) could end up owning lands where the ranchers were currently grazing their livestock so cheaply. James Watt declared the Sagebrush Rebellion "over" when he took office as secretary of the interior in 1981; he underlined its lack of necessity by maintaining the policies of the past — livestock numbers on public lands continued at previous quotas, and grazing fees were actually reduced. Whereas in 1980 the fee for grazing a thousand-pound cow for one month had been $2.36, by 1983 it was $1.40.

"It's hard to think of anything less democratic," Eben said as he opened the gate (which was unlocked). "After the Temblor controversy in 1960, grazing fees went way up here. Then, when Reagan came in, they were cut in half. But I don't mind Reagan — he's just a pimp for private interests. He was picked and brought up and trained just like a race-horse. He's an entrepreneur, and he's going to go as far as he can. It isn't his strength that lets him get away with it; it's our weakness."

The controversy that Eben mentioned concerned overgrazing in the Temblors. Despite (or, ironically, because of) their aridity, these mountains had historically been a thriving upland game habitat, filled with quail and partridge — a place where Eben and his brothers and their friends often went to camp and hunt. Much of this habitat had been grazed off by the middle of this century, though the higher elevations of the dehydrated southern part of the range still retained some shrub cover because of the utter absence of water for stock. In the fall of 1958, however, a pipeline was introduced into this part of the range, and water troughs and sheep quickly followed. A confederation of local sportsmen's and conservation groups formed (including the McMillans and coordinated by one Dr. Enrico Bongio of California Polytechnic College in San Luis Obispo), urging that stockwater developments on BLM lands in the Temblor Range be halted. Eventually 58,000 acres, referred to as the Temblor Land and Wildlife Management Area, were withdrawn for study and protection, but the controversy continued for several years, producing, among other things, an extraordinary series of letters in the local newspapers. This one appeared on November 17, 1961, in the *Paso Robles Press:*

> The press and radio of the county have recently carried a number of stories on the terribly overgrazed and distressed condition of the Temblor Range. At the suggestion of a number of neighbors, I'm writing to assure the people of the cities and towns of the County that things are not quite that bad, lest they start sending us Care packages and organizing emergency relief committees. . . .
>
> There is an old saying that a little learning is a dangerous thing. It is one that I think all of us, including Dr. Bongio, should repeat several times every morning. It is apparent that the organized sportsmen who are speaking in such dogmatic fashion on the Temblor Range know little or nothing about its xerophytic flora; a flora that is one of the most dra-

matic features of the arid southern Temblor Range and the upper San Joaquin Valley. This flora, whose ancestry dates back millions of years, developed in response to the increasing aridity of southwestern North America since the close of Cretaceous time. In other words, Dr. Bongio, the sheep and cattle didn't do it all in 10 or 12 years — some of the things of which you complain have been developing for at least 70 million.

People who have open minds soon realize that they must forget what they have learned in regions of normal rainfall when they enter our land of little rain. For nothing is quite what the books say it should be. Disturbed soil, quite undesirable in the regions the textbooks are based on, is essential for the successful germination and growth of many arid region plants, including the most colorful native wildflowers. (These wildflowers, although of little interest to the shotgun boys, have at times attracted national attention to the Temblor Range; they are at their sensational best in the first wet year after several dry ones have left the soil sufficiently blown, drifted, and barren.)

Then, too, it is a flora closely associated with and dependent upon grazing. Kit Carson in the 1830's, Bishop Kip and Lt. Williamson in the 1850's, and finally Mary Austin in the 1880's and '90's, have all reported on the tremendous number of antelope, elk, and other wildlife found in the upper San Joaquin Valley and its surrounding arid ranges. While I know the experts of the sportsmen's groups will disagree with me, even so, I have a strong feeling these animals must have eaten something.

I could go on at some length on this subject of xerophytic floras, a favorite of mine (such a favorite that it has led me to making, so far, 6,701 scientific plant collections in the arid regions). But, then, I'm just a rancher, and one of the most important points I gather from the recent publicity is that the ranchers really don't know very much about their ranges, even though they have successfully lived and paid taxes on them for several generations.

As for the so-called Temblor Public Range, one wonders why all the sudden interest in some of the most arid, barren, and God-forsaken ridges in central California. I don't think any of the resident ranchers would complain much if the southern Temblor desert public lands are closed to all grazing — so long as they were also closed to all hunting. One wonders if Dr. Bongio and his colleagues, perhaps unwittingly, are just a front for an ever-expanding bureaucracy. The Bureau of Land Management has now withdrawn 58,000 acres of public land from possible conversion to private ownership, foreclosing forever the possibility that it may get on the local tax rolls, where much of it belongs. This land has been turned over to the California State Department of Fish and Game for a public hunting playground. The Fish and Game Commission, incredible as it may seem in an allegedly free society, now has the power to condemn private land for public hunting grounds. I suspect the Shotgun Lobby, for which Dr. Bongio seems to be the spokesman, is merely furnishing the propaganda for a move by the Fish and Game Commission to condemn large blocks of privately-owned Temblor grazing lands. But I have no right to speculate on motives (although one does hear things). All I really know is that the spokesmen for this group have a great deal of pretty basic stuff to learn about the geology, botany, evolution, grazing, erosion, floristics, zoology, economy, taxation, and other allied phenomena of arid regions. As one with a sincere but realistic interest in conservation, I also wish they'd learn a little about good public relations for conservationists.

But, to quote an old reporter's maxim, an ounce of publicity is worth a pound of merit. And they certainly are getting the publicity — it's too bad so much of the merit got lost along the way.

Ernest Twisselmann

Ernest Twisselmann was the brother of Eben and Ian's brother-in-law Carl. He was also the author of *Flora of the*

Temblor Range and the Neighboring Part of the San Joaquin Valley.
He was born in Cholame, near Eben's ranch, in 1917 and
died there in 1972; in between, he graduated from the University of California at Berkeley and spent most of his life as
a cattle rancher. In 1952, after an outbreak of nitrate poisoning decimated the ranks of California cattle, Twisselmann
set out "to interpret the strange and bewildering botanical
names of plants known to concentrate lethal nitrate com-
pounds." At Eben's urging, he sought the assistance of John
Thomas Howell of the California Academy of Sciences, who
told him that in order to analyze the plants on his family's
ranchlands in the Temblor region he should collect them
and record their localities. Twisselmann followed this advice
beyond any and all expectations, effectively launching a second career and eventually becoming a respected name in
California botany; his books (*Flora of Kern County,* published
in 1968, later analyzed 1,875 species and varieties of vascular
plants in one of the most floristically diverse regions of one of
the most floristically diverse states in the union) differ from
most floras in that they offer exhaustive information on habitat and distribution rather than formal botanical keys or
descriptions. They also contain many original observations
of the sort that characterize his letter, to which Dr. Bongio
responded on November 22, 1961:

> I cannot bring myself to believe that Mr. Twisselmann's
> feelings on this matter are shared by the rank and file stock-
> men of this area. He refers to our county-wide sportsman
> and conservation groups as the "Shotgun Lobby" and by
> sly innuendo places us in a low class group of dupes working
> for some mythical group of bureaucrats. It is none of my
> business how a private land owner manages his land or af-
> fairs. It is my business however to ask for a closer look into
> the land use or abuse as it pertains to our public ranges
> throughout the nation. . . .

Perhaps Mr. Twisselmann was not aware that under the provisions of the recent congressional action setting aside various tracts of public lands in California, there will be stock grazing (continuing under the present low grazing fee of 23 cents per animal unit per month), mining, lumbering, etc., just as before, BUT now the wildlife has been recognized as a beneficial user of these resources. It is felt that the State Department of Fish and Game may be better able to manage these wildlife resources without fear of having the land slip into private ownership. Now it seems there are still a few of us around who consider our wildlife as a valuable and cherished asset rather than something which some way or another must be put up with. If it is a crime to aid in trying to provide conditions conducive to desirable wildlife habitat, then I for one stand convicted. . . .

It was reassuring to find one as qualified as Mr. Twisselmann to admit "the ranges have been fairly heavily grazed." In addition his suggestion that all hunting as well as all grazing be brought to a halt on this public range deserves a long second look. If this could be arranged, I can see no reason for the recently installed $36,000 watering system along the upper range. . . .

Of special interest to me was Mr. Twisselmann's report on the range conditions which sustained "tremendous numbers of antelope, elk, and other wildlife found in the upper San Joaquin Valley and its surrounding arid regions" between 1830 and 1890. What has happened to the obvious growth required to sustain this flourishing herd??? Could it be that the sheep grazing pressure of the past 70 years has had a detrimental effect on this general area??? It seems that man in many cases is his own worst enemy. . . .

At any rate, let's keep the letters pouring in on this important topic, and please, drop the Dr., it's just plain

Mr. Enrico P. Bongio

Ian McMillan answered Bongio's parting exhortation with this oratorical letter to the "Voice of the People" column of the *San Luis Obispo Telegram Tribune:*

On its own public ranges and at public expense our society actually supports a program of land ruin and depletion. The lessees of grazing privileges on those public lands pay a mere pittance of rental, which in 1960 amounted to 22 cents per month per cow unit of pasturage. This, in a typical case, amounted to less than half of the taxes paid on adjoining private holdings, and less than one-tenth of what was charged for the same amount of pasturage on private range in the same vicinity. On an investigated area, no evidence was found that the federal regulations limiting grazing on this BLM range were enforced or complied with. Restriction of animal units to comply with range capacity and units paid for was not in evidence. The attitude of BLM range officials toward this ruinous grazing has been one of approval, protection, and promotion. Through a law which requires the refunding of grazing fees to the county where collected, these fees, when used as specified, are actually returned to the range lessees in the form of payments of normal costs of grazing operations such as water developments, fencing, predator control. This amazing setup operates under a provision of the federal Taylor Grazing Act, which allows local advisory boards, comprised overwhelmingly of lessees who grace the public range, to exercise a free hand in ruling and dominating the administration of that range.

The public pays for treating infestations of noxious weeds, rodents, and insect plagues that occur on those ranges as direct consequences of land abuse. It pays for a costly program of fire protection on areas where excessive grazing has stripped off everything that would burn. It pays for wildlife management programs that are nullified by ruinous grazing practices. It pays for a federal program of poisoning and trapping of coyotes, bobcats, badgers, and other valuable wildlife solely to protect sheep on these ranges, and it pays a subsidy on the wool marketed. It allows imported alien sheep herders to be worked on these ranges under feudalistic conditions of indentured servitude such as our nation claims to be free of and opposed to. It pays a growing army of bureaucrats to administer this incredible program.

Official range technicians on the public domain, assuming the role of philosophers and scientists, interpret the immediate, temporary results of their burning, bulldozing, spraying, fertilizing, reseeding experiments as evidence of "improvement" and "development." These short-sighted misconceptions are then used to promote range practices that only serve to further facilitate and accelerate the ruin already in progress. This official outlook when further subverted by the economically possessed grazing interest, has brought forth some most amazing attitudes toward land use. It explains the astounding behavior of prominent, influential and well-educated stockmen who, while standing in the midst of range devastation and depletion, adamantly defend, approve and recommend such conditions. This affiliation between the ecologically illiterate, economically dominated grazing interest, and the public agencies in charge of range research is the controlling factor in the grazing problem on our public domain.

Ian I. McMillan

Ian's reference to the "astounding behavior of prominent, influential and well-educated stockmen" was an obvious swipe at Twisselmann, who responded on December 5:

Before turning to Mr. Bongio's problems, I should like to comment briefly on Mr. Ian McMillan's letter of yesterday. I don't know who the "prominent, influential and well-educated" stockmen may be. I suppose some of the stockmen of eastern San Luis Obispo and western Kern County really are prominent, influential, and well-educated, although I doubt that any of them ordinarily think of themselves in such flattering terms. But I wonder if it is just possible that Mr. McMillan might be wrong and that the reason that they have these qualities is that they are pretty shrewd, learned, and savvy, or they wouldn't have survived all these years in a most rigorous and demanding way of life and still have time to become "prominent, well-educated, and influential." At any rate, it seems logical to at least listen to them; if I wanted to learn all about, let's say, newspapers in San Luis Obispo, I would go first to a publisher or editor, not to an instructor of, let's say, blacksmithing at Cal Poly.

When he says "prominent, well-educated, and influential," I know there is nothing personal about it, as even my best friends would be appalled at the mere thought of using any of these words to describe me. But "ecologically illiterate" — that's me, for sure! Years ago, when I first got interested in all these matters, I knew all the answers to all the questions. On the most profound and involved problems I could be just as dogmatic and positive as Mr. McMillan and Mr. Bongio. But now, after spending all the time possible for several years exploring every nook and cranny of Kern County, I'll have to admit that it has been a losing battle and that I know next to nothing about the larger questions of region ecology. I have found out one thing, however — never dismiss too quickly the opinion of the man on the ground. Mr. McMillan and Mr. Bongio might be astonished at how much knowledge people like cowboys, sheepherders, lumberjacks, prospectors, and forest rangers sometimes have.

While I rarely defend bureaucrats, I think Mr. McMillan in all fairness should have included just a few more facts about the Bakersfield office of the Bureau of Land Management. . . . In the 1958–61 period, with which he is concerned there was a maximum of five field men charged with all the details of administering "fourteen million" acres of public land in the 13 southern counties. It is clear, even to those of us who are ecologically and otherwise illiterate that if this skeleton staff had done even a portion of what Mr. McMillan and his associates wanted them to do with the Temblor Public Range, they would have had to virtually ignore the other thirteen million nine hundred forty two thousand acres. It seems to me that if he has a complaint, it should be with the United States Congress for not budgeting more money to the agency so that it might be adequately staffed. Perhaps if the fantastic amounts of money given to wheat farmers who put their farms in the soil bank had been used for more worthwhile purposes, we would all have less to complain about. . . .

Now, to Mr. Bongio. In my own recent letter, I mentioned the tremendous number of antelope and elk the upper San Joaquin Valley and its surrounding ranges once supported. He asked, "What has happened to the obvious growth required to sustain these animals? Could it be that the sheep grazing pressure of the past 70 years has had a detrimental effect on this range?"

The answer is, nope. On the lowlands, it has been converted to many thousands of acres of, among other things, cotton, potatoes, sugar peas, pears, oranges, alfalfa, permanent pasture, castor beans, rice, and watermelons. On the uplands and in the surrounding ranges, it supports thousands of cattle and sheep, on lands varying from desert ridges to well developed woodland. In local areas, there are turkeys, wheat, barley, rye, and seed grass, alfalfa, and carrots. In addition the private property owner in the upland region also furnishes, without cost to the taxpayer, the forage and water for thousands of black-tailed and mule deer, quail, doves, and other wildlife; and also bears the quite considerable cost, irritation, and even occasional danger of physical injury involved in protecting this wildlife from the "sportsmen" of the cities and towns.

And — I almost forgot — the region where the elk and antelope used to roam also now supports a human population of more than 300,000.

Mr. Bongio would probably prefer it the way it was in 1880; so would I. That is why I choose to live out in this "barren," "overgrazed," "windswept" region, so far from some center of culture and sophistication such as San Luis Obispo. But then I would prefer to have San Luis Obispo restored to its "natural" state, too, and see it become once

more a pleasant place of marshes, meadows, and woods, no-
table chiefly for a huge population of grizzly bears.

Mr. Bongio then questions my assertion that the Fish and
Game Commission has the power to condemn private land
under the State's power of eminent domain. . . . On the
narrowest of technicalities, he might be correct — such
condemnation would probably be brought in the name of
the State of California or the County of San Luis Obispo,
rather than in the name of the Fish and Game Commission
as such. And the ostensible reason might be something quite
different from the real one — the reason often used is "to
protect the watershed" . . . regardless of the ostensible reason, many thousands of acres of private land now open to
public hunting and fishing were acquired by condemnation
proceedings. One lawyer told me I must have flunked my
seventh grade civics course, or I would have known that the
inherent right of the State to condemn land for the "public
good" is almost unlimited. . . . (Only recently, the Navy at-
tempted to condemn the entire Temblor for a bombing
range. Let me assure you, our fears of these possibilities are
by no means "mythical.")

As long as I have taken this much space to answer the
question directed to me, and as this is my final letter on the
subject, I may as well make a few additional comments on
Mr. Bongio's letter.

"Fear of having the land slip into private ownership." I
suppose this is basically a political, rather than a biological
question. However, there may be thousands of tax-payers in
San Luis Obispo County . . . who would be anything but
"fearful" of having an extra 58,000 acres added to their tax
base. (Various governmental agencies now own more than
50 percent of all land in California.)

"Barren windswept areas." There is no point dwelling on
this, but by the time fall comes, most of the slopes of the
southern Temblor are by nature barren and windswept, a
common characteristic of arid ranges. But even if this were
not so, one might as well be realistic and let the sheep and

cattle graze it off. For if the public range is ever developed as a hunting reserve of any real significance, it will almost inevitably be burned off by the time hunting season is over, anyhow.

"Admits the range is fairly heavily grazed." I didn't admit anything — after three dry years all of California, from Tecate, San Diego County, to Likely, Modoc County, is fairly heavily grazed. I'm surprised that this is considered news.

In passing, I regret any mistaken impression readers may have that these letters have been some sort of feud. On the contrary, it is a refreshing change to discuss grazing xerophily, ecology, and such with a spokesman for the sportsmen. This is especially true for one who is usually occupied with less enlightened sports in fixing fences they have cut, repairing holes they have shot in tanks, mourning non-game wildlife they have shot for target practice, picking up beer cans they have strewn, and buying new locks to replace the ones they have smashed. Perhaps we can even hope that a new day is dawning, when they will get their kicks from observing, studying fauna, instead of killing it. When that day arrives, we will take their concern about conservation a great deal more seriously.

In later, private notes and letters, Twisselmann said that he thought it was almost impossible to overgraze annual vegetation and observed that native plants seemed to tolerate grazing very well. "Recreation is now by far the greatest enemy of conservation," he wrote. "I strongly feel, so far as our own region is concerned, that the only hope for the wild lands below the yellow pine belt is private ownership with well-locked gates and surly land-owners." In his advocacy of private enterprise and his distrust of tax-supported bureaucracy, Twisselmann's political orientation is obvious; but the striking thing about the entire series of letters (aside from the humor, intelligence, and ease with which these ranchers expressed themselves) is not their reflection of predictable ideologies but rather their vivid illustration of the complexity of environmental positions. Hunters are popularly assigned a place on the right wing of outdoors enthusiasts, yet the conservative Twisselmann despised them. Ian attacked BLM officials — administrators of publicly held land whom one might have expected him to support. Twisselmann defended these same bureaucrats, whose jobs he would have preferred to see terminated. In all, the letters support the notion that environmentalism is extrapolitical — especially when someone as conservative as Twisselmann is considered a leading conservationist.

"Ernest Twisselmann was kind of a genius," Eben remarked. We had now reached the top of the Temblors and were surrounded by plunging red-brown ridges spotted with juniper, marked by symmetrical vertical protrusions that looked like dinosaur claws. Spread before us was the white, sandy surrounding country — the Carrizo stretching away to the west, the lifeless-looking San Joaquin Valley oil fields below us to the east, with flat grids of parched towns lying dead in the dull brown desert. "He was a very intelligent fella to have been born and raised by a ranching family. He'd been in training for the diplomatic corps, but he got TB, and after that his family got after him: 'Ernest! Don't lift that!' 'Ernest! Don't go out without your coat!' It got to the point where he was stoop-shouldered from all the invectives that were on him. He used to pick my two oldest boys up from school just for companionship; one of them said something to him about atriplex one day, and he started thinking about how nobody in his family could tell one plant from another. After he got interested in botany, people from the city started stopping by; his family would think they wanted to buy cattle, but they'd say, 'No, I came to see Ernest Twisselmann.' It gave him some dignity and stature. He was a very scholarly person. Later on he changed his mind about overgrazing — he admitted that some plants had disappeared."

We drove home in gathering dusk — down the Temblors, through the gate, east and north of Soda Lake, past a place in the northern Carrizo where the Fluor Corporation had installed 160 acres' worth of solar generators. Eben said, "If somebody asked me whether I'd rather have Hodgkin's disease, leprosy, or a stomach ulcer, I'd probably take the stomach ulcer, figuring I'd stand a pretty good chance of getting through. That's how I feel about solar energy. You never get something for nothing; what worries me is finding out what we're finally going to have to pay for solar power. We don't understand what happens to the ground that isn't receiving the sunlight."

When we got back to the ranch, I went to wash up in the guest cabin. One comment from the letters nagged at me. Twisselmann advised, "Never dismiss too quickly the opinion of the man on the ground"; but what exactly did he consider the McMillans? City slickers? Cloud dwellers? For that matter, what role had Eben played in the Temblor controversy? None of the published letters had been written by him; where did he and Twisselmann stand, especially after he'd helped launch Twisselmann's illustrious botanical career?

Later, I obtained a copy of Twisselmann's *Flora of Kern County,* whose title page includes the inscription: "Illustrated by Eben and Gladys McMillan." Then I came across another letter that had been written to the *Telegram Tribune.* Twisselmann, responding to yet another attack, wrote: "I think conservation exemplified by such things as Mr. Eben McMillan's award-winning motion picture 'The Shandon Hills' will achieve far more than all the ill-considered charges and counter-charges that have been thrown about."

"We always disagreed just for the sake of argument," said Eben, who, by the time I got up to the house for dinner, had looked up the mallow from Grant's Lake — the one he hadn't been able to identify but guessed would have grown in the lakebed before the arrival of white men. He showed me its entry in his flora. It said that the mallow was found in "low wet places and alkali flats." *Sida hederacea:* a native species.

Eben's ancestors emigrated from Scotland in the 1820s, toward the end of the time known as the clearances. Until then, poor Highlands farmers had worked small communal plots of land called run-rigs; given their primitive plowing methods and rocky, unproductive soil, not much in the way of a crop could be taken from these holdings, and, beginning at the end of the eighteenth century, the Scottish lairds — encouraged by the English crown, which had previously destroyed the clans — cleared the crofters out, replacing them with sheep. The McMillans' home — the 23-mile-long isle of Arran, in the Firth of Clyde in the Inner Hebrides — was owned by the duke of Hamilton, who made the magnanimous gesture of bestowing one pound upon every Highlander who left.

Like all of the clans, the McMillans dispersed. Some of

them made a go of it in the Lowlands; others departed for Australia and America. One McMillan, Daniel, got a job in a Glasgow bookshop and eventually started his own business, the Macmillan Publishing Company. His grandson Harold had the most success in dealing with the jurisdiction of England, becoming prime minister of the country. A more typical course was followed by Donald, who — in company with other McMillans, McNairs, Cooks, Whites, Stuarts, and Fergusons — landed at the Bay of Chaleur, in Restigouche County, New Brunswick, in the autumn of 1829. Without any time to build houses before winter, the immigrants tunneled into the hillsides and boarded up the openings. Eastern Canadian weather is less forgiving than that of the Inner Hebrides, whose chilly dampness is at least mitigated by the influence of the Gulf Stream; nevertheless, these stubborn Scots stayed in New Brunswick — logging, fishing, and farming soil as poor as that to which they were accustomed on Arran — for four decades. But ultimately even they succumbed to the lure responsible for so much of modern North American history.

In 1867, the Cooks departed for California. They sailed from St. John to New York City and from there to Central America; upon landing in Panama, they were informed that transportation across the isthmus would cost twice their passage from New York. While trying to come to terms with this dilemma, they were robbed of most of their belongings. So they took the only course left to them — they walked from the Caribbean to the Pacific, the men carrying the smaller children, in the only clothes they had: woolens woven by generations of women whose sole climatic experience had been gained on the shores of the North Atlantic. When they finally reached San Francisco, they went to inquire about work at a hotel where Gaelic was spoken and were overheard by a man who introduced himself as Captain McDonald; he said that he owned a steamship company and a sheep ranch to the south. When he asked if they had any experience with wool, even their inbred Presbyterian reserve could not keep the Cooks from laughing.

As it turned out, Captain McDonald owned most of the Carrizo Plain. When the Cooks went there, they took their three younger daughters with them and left the older three to work in San Francisco. One of the latter was sixteen-year-old Elizabeth, whose departure from New Brunswick had wrenched the heart of young Donald C. McMillan. After the golden spike was driven (the one in the railroad after the one in his heart), "D.C." took a steamer to Quebec and a train to the West Coast, arriving in San Francisco in 1872.

Donald and Lizzie would eventually marry, but for the moment there was a frontier to exploit, so in the spring D.C. left for the Sierra Nevada to cut timber for the mines and the railroad. When he finally made it south to Shandon, he was awestruck by what he saw; the region was being farmed for the first time, and the crops were so heavy that they collapsed under their own weight. Back in New Brunswick, where the ground was still frozen solid, the family received word that Donald had found the Garden of Eden. Before long, other McMillans began leaving Canada for California.

By the time D.C.'s brother Jim arrived from British Columbia, Donald had opened a general store in Cayucos, where steamships docked on the San Luis Obispo County coast. Jim was watching boats being unloaded on a November day in 1884 when his other brother, Alexander, came walking up the gangplank, having made the trip from New Brunswick unannounced. That winter Jim and Alex traveled inland to visit friends who lived in a canyon near Shandon, which then consisted of a post office, a school, a church, a store, a blacksmith shop, and a hotel with a bar. They had to sleep in a haystack on a freezing night, but they still liked the place so much that they filed patents on homesteads in the canyon. Seven members of the McMillan family eventually acquired adjoining properties there. After their children married or reached school age, most of them moved closer to the coast; only one stayed in what came to be called McMillan Canyon. That was Alex — Eben's and Ian's father.

According to Ian, Alexander McMillan was "a great man in an era when greatness was taken for granted — he could run a harvester, doctor a sick cow, preach a sermon, raise a family, and win an election." As to the last, for a time Alex served as a Democratic state assemblyman from eastern San Luis Obispo County (there has been only one since). As for the sermons, while he wasn't overly religious — unlike most of his peers — he was humanitarian, and he was frequently called upon to administer the last rites when a neighbor died. Alex functioned as a community arbiter, often helping to settle arguments and lending support to families with problems. If there was a dispute over a debt or a fence line, if someone's husband was drinking too much, if a rancher's cattle had contracted some mysterious malady, the aggrieved citizen would appear in McMillan Canyon and consult with Alexander into the night. Eben recalls a number of times when he left for town with his father, only to run into someone Alex knew, talk to him for a couple of hours, and finally turn around and go home without ever getting near town. When he did succeed in reaching civilization, Alex would go first to the post office, buy a newspaper, roll it up, and brandish it like a baton as he discoursed with acquaintances on the street. He never carried a weapon, assuming that if he were ever threatened he would be able to talk sense into his assailant.

"Being noncompetitive, he didn't have any enemies," says Eben. "He was a poor businessman — he never invested in anything. If he had ten dollars, anybody who was hungry would get it." Whenever Alex went to the bank, he would bring home a hobo, who would stay at the house for a couple of days and, as a memento, leave a batch of "graybacks" behind. "My mother made us boil the bedclothes every time those guys came through," Eben says.

Such fastidiousness was not altogether typical of Eben's mother, Mary Frances Harte McMillan, who by all accounts was not terribly interested in housework. Once a neighbor child visited the McMillans and asked what the webs were up in the corners; Alex said they were Irish lace. (Fran — as Mrs. McMillan's friends called her — was Irish.) Alex cooked most of the meals; Fran preferred making custards and cakes. You might say she had no taste for the mundane, which is perhaps understandable in someone who could speak both French and Italian, had been trained to sing light opera (she had a clear, sweet soprano voice), and played the piano, French horn, and guitar.

Fran had gone to college in San Jose and come to Shandon to teach grammar school. She met Alex when she took a room in the home of his brother and sister-in-law. When Fran and Alex had their first child — a boy, Gordon — Fran's mother had him baptized a Catholic; the McMillans, of course, were strictly Presbyterian. Soon afterward, Fran had the first of a series of breakdowns that would recur throughout her life. Her "brain fever," as the family referred to it, apparently involved hallucinations and was usually brought on by some cataclysmic event; one of Fran's spells of delirium was triggered when a local man fell to his death from a balloon at a picnic. She would become hyperactive, then withdrawn. One time, in a fit, she swam the Shandon River; on another occasion she showed up at the schoolhouse *sans costume*. When he couldn't restrain her, Alex took Fran to the county courthouse, where her answers to the judge's questions were so quick-witted that pretty soon she *and* the judge were cracking up. For want of a better diagnosis, she was defined as schizophrenic and spent three weeks at a San

Jose mental hospital, returning there three times in later years.

Fran liked to read and write. She knew the spelling and derivation of practically every word in the dictionary, and she insisted that words be pronounced phonetically (which is probably why Ian pronounces his name "*Eye*-an"). She had her brother Lou — whose wife was a member of the Salvation Army in San Diego — send boxes of books and copies of the *National Geographic* and *Saturday Evening Post* to Shandon. Ignorance angered her, and when she developed a special interest — in the Russian Revolution, say — she made sure that her family found out about it. She could hold forth on a topic all day and (according to Eben's brother Don) could also "nicely give people the word and shut them up." This proved a useful gift, as anything that happened in McMillan Canyon inspired a full family colloquy. The children would gather around the woodstove, each expatiating with enthusiasm; Alex would listen politely from the corner, blowing smoke rings from his cigar. Finally he would deliver a pronouncement, usually lofty. The next day Fran would lecture the kids and "bring Alex down to earth."

Eben's sister Dorothy says she can't remember either of her parents ever using the word "good" or "bad." Neither did they talk about love or show affection to one another. Love was invoked in the broader sense — the brotherly kind, the type that venerated God's creatures. Fran was a woman who would lecture a man for beating his horse in front of her children; she went for long walks and knew the names of the wildflowers. She wrote that the Shandon region

was a beautiful clean land of hills and practically virgin soil backed by the pure, blue line of the coast range mountains and overarched by the equally unsullied blue of the clear western sky. The grassy slopes were starred with wildflowers and the valleys were dotted with stately oaks forming mag-

nificent parks and avenues, casting a spell of silence that at
once strangely exalted and humbled the beholder. . . . The
blue skies said freedom and the nesting hills said home.

It's difficult to characterize California in that era without
sounding ridiculously romantic. Facts sound like exaggera-
tions. Farmers would drag a tree limb over the land as a
plow, throw a handful of grain after it, and get three generations of crops from the single planting. When the Southern
Pacific Railroad first reached from the north into the Salinas
Valley, it brought a wheat boom to the grasslands around
Shandon; in a few years, the area's grain output increased by
literally 1,000 percent. Bells hung from the wheat wagons
that took grain to the train, and in Ian's mind, "the spirit of
the whole pioneer movement was dramatically echoed in the
sound of these team bells." (They might also be construed to
have been tolling for condors, which disappeared as their primary food sources — deer, elk, and later livestock — were
replaced by waving fields of wheat.)

The road that followed McMillan Canyon was used as a
cattle trail by ranchers moving their herds to market, and as
boys Eben and Ian would watch a dozen vaqueros, whooping and whistling in sombreros and spurs, drive hundreds of
half-wild steers past their house. "Their horses had fire coming out of their eyes, but they could control them with their
little finger," Eben says with admiration. These Spanish
cowboys were a ranch kid's rock 'n' roll stars — larger than
life, flamboyant and free. When telephone lines were strung
up around Shandon, a vaquero by the name of Juan Cer-
vantes rode along shooting the glass insulators from the
poles. One time when Eben's older brother and sister accidentally set fire to a hillside — they were surreptitiously trying to light cigarettes — a vaquero called Victor Ortega
appeared out of nowhere to extinguish the flames with his
coiled riata.

Eben and Ian each left school after the ninth grade. When the McMillan children — five boys and two girls — weren't in class, they were in the hills: running jackrabbits, chasing coyotes, looking for rattlesnakes, catching tarantulas. Eben and Ian had a pair of donkeys that they had trained to go under fences so that they could ride through the entire countryside without opening a gate. Once, on their way to school, they were chased by a gang of vaqueros ("just for devilment, mainly") but escaped as soon as the assailants' horses encountered their first fence. The McMillan boys slept in an old cabin across the road from the family's main house and were therefore the envy of all their friends. The cabin had no windows, but it did have a pool table. The walls were covered with pictures of prizefighters and birds from boxes of Arm & Hammer baking soda. ("Unfortunately," says Eben, "most of them were eastern species.") Guessing games consisted of questions like: "I'm thinking of an animal with a long tail and a hooked beak . . ." Animals were a hot topic, not least because of the food source they represented.

As soon as the boys were old enough, they became hunters. "Prowess with a gun was a mark of high distinction," Ian later wrote in *Man and the California Condor*. "Wildlife of whatever species was commonly shot on sight. The more uncommon or rare the target, the more quick and eager was the shooting." This was the era when the grizzly and antelope disappeared throughout most of California, and the condor was closer to extinction then than it would be forty years later. There was actually an ongoing trade in the birds' skins, and collectors would pay $250 for a single condor egg. To make that kind of money through normal channels, Kelly Truesdale would have had to pitch hay for the better part of a year.

Kelly Truesdale was a member of one of Shandon's first pioneer families. According to Ian, the Truesdales were really more tribe than family; there were a lot of local jokes about just how many of them there were. Two of the Truesdale boys, for example, were identical twins who married identical twin sisters. Kelly was considered a halfwit because he didn't like to work and he tended to mumble. If you spent a day with him and didn't say anything, he wouldn't say anything either. "But around a campfire," Eben says, "he was a good conversationalist." Truesdale lived in abandoned houses, showing up every spring ("like the wildflowers") smelling of sagebrush and chewing tobacco, in later years driving a four-cylinder Buick with an eagle for a hood ornament. He made his living by collecting and selling rare eggs, and if he needed help reaching a nest, he'd come by and pick up one of the McMillan boys. Sometimes they would be away from home for as long as a month. "Traveling the back ranges and valleys of the big ranches, visiting the cliffs where ravens and prairie falcons nested, searching the woodlands of pine and oak for the high nests of golden eagles, we continually learned about the local bird life and its nesting habits," Ian wrote. "We were learning the principles and workings of ecology long before the new science was heard of in the condor country."

It was on a trip with Truesdale that Eben, at the age of thirteen, saw his first condors. "We'd climbed up on top of this rock — Kelly was like a danged spider, he only weighed about a hundred and twenty pounds. He even *walked* like an animal, always zigzagging and stopping to look behind him. He'd trace an animal that was trying to throw him off just like a detective would go after a murderer. 'They're trying to bamboozle me,' he'd say. We were lying in the brush, trying to keep from being seen, and all of a sudden Kelly whooped: '*There they are!*' Seven condors came in and circled right around us. Jeez, it was like an electric shock — after hearing all these stories and asking Kelly what condors looked like.

Actually, they weren't near as big as I thought they'd be; Kelly'd made it sound like there'd be a big circus tent floating up in the sky."

Kelly himself had seen his first condor in 1907, the year Eben was born. He was pitching hay on the Carrizo Plain, and the bird's unmistakable shadow passed within a few feet of him. Truesdale looked up and watched the condor diminish in size until it disappeared into a canyon in the La Panza Mountains. He made a mental note of the spot. The following February, he and a friend chopped a trail through the chaparral and found condors nesting high in a sheer wall of rock. Kelly climbed the cliff, flushed the adult condor from the nest, and found a four-and-a-half-inch egg — the biggest he'd ever seen. He wrapped it in cotton, placed it in a coffee can, and returned to Shandon a hero. Only one or two local people had ever even seen a condor.

Truesdale drained the contents of the egg and put it up for sale. He received a response from one W. Lee Chambers, a resident of Santa Monica, salesman of hunting rifles, and business manager of the Cooper Ornithological Club. Truesdale met Chambers in Paso Robles, the nearest town on the railroad. To Kelly's astonishment, the influential birdman refused the egg; he said that its creamy white color didn't have the light green tinge that characterized condor eggs, intimating that it was the product of a swan. In desperation Truesdale sent letters all over the country. Eventually he received an offer of $300 — contingent on proof of the egg's authenticity — from John E. Thayer, a wealthy Massachusetts collector who already owned seven condor eggs.

For two years Kelly watched the nest. (Undisturbed condors lay only one egg every other year on the bare floor of their cave; this minimalist approach — the lowest reproductive rate of any North American bird, necessitated by an eighteen-month-long period of juvenile dependency — is one factor that has depressed the wild population.) When it appeared that the condors were again nesting, Thayer dispatched William Leon Dawson — the ornithologist who would soon author *The Birds of California* — to Shandon. Cheered by the townspeople, Dawson, Truesdale, and Gordon McMillan set out for the nest in April. It took them a day and a half to cover the 30 miles to the site; they camped overnight at the foot of the bluff, saw condors entering the nest, and the next morning climbed the cliff. When they got near the cavity, they heard a grunt. Truesdale looked inside the cave and saw a downy gray condor chick huddled against the far wall. The object of the trip and of two years' waiting — the egg — was no more.

In despair, Truesdale threw a pebble at the nestling. It moved out of the way, revealing a light-colored scrap on the floor. Ignoring the hissing chick, Kelly scrambled into the cave and fetched the fragment: a piece of creamy white eggshell. Dawson took a long look at it and agreed to certify the original egg as that of a condor. The $300 that Truesdale received was the most money ever paid for a condor egg. He took four more from the same nest over the next decade.

Laws prohibiting the shooting of condors and the collection of their eggs existed even then, but as Kelly Truesdale's exploits attest, these rules were roundly ignored. "Shooting at a condor was like spitting in the street," Eben says. "Birds weren't important. If you stole a horse they'd hang you without any trial, but they'd never think of putting somebody in jail just for having a buzzard egg." At least seventy condor eggs are known to have been collected between 1859 and 1943, mostly around the turn of the century, a time of intense interest in natural history in America. A contemporary survey of natural history museums found 177 California condor specimens; one example of how such specimens were obtained is offered by the San Diego Natural History Museum, which in 1925 was anonymously given a fresh condor carcass — on the condition that no questions be asked.

People were killing condors in North America long before the arrival of Europeans. American Indians, who worshiped the condor's propensities for holding up the world, creating thunder and lightning, and controlling solar and lunar eclipses, slayed the bird as part of a burial rite. To them the condor, with its ability to soar into the uppermost reaches of the world after feeding on the shells of departed spirits, was a messenger from the living to the dead. Still, it's doubtful that Indian rituals, even conducted over several more centuries, would have reduced the bird to its present ranks. Modern facts lend an eerie prophecy to the first European record of a California condor sighting. At Monterey Bay in 1602, Father Antonio de la Ascension (the same friar who so admired the frameless canoe of the Chumash) saw a group of condors feeding on a dead whale — an appropriate herald for the arrival of Caucasians. The first "American" record was made by Lewis and Clark, who encountered several condors above the cascades of the Columbia. Lewis tried to shoot one and missed; but the following winter, of 1805–6, the party succeeded in bagging four. Within forty years, condors had disappeared from the region.

The Scottish naturalist David Douglas, who visited Oregon in 1826, noted that condor feathers were popular for use in the stems of tobacco pipes. Most contemporary chroniclers maintain that the feathers were also used in California as containers for gold dust, though there's hardly any reference to this practice in Gold Rush literature. Much the most pertinent factor in the history of man's relationship with the condor is the irrational ethic epitomized by Alonzo Winship, a Pony Express rider who, in 1854, came upon a sleeping condor near his cabin in the Sierra. Winship was surprised that the bird had not been awakened by his approach, so he threw his shovel at it and broke its wing.

Today we wonder why people were so moved to exterminate a creature that was neither edible nor predatory. One factor, undoubtedly, was the unpopular image of a vulture. Even more inflammatory was the condor's size; on any wilderness frontier, a big animal was a symbol of elements that had to be overcome. Early California settlers erroneously suspected that condors carried off calves, lambs, and children. As noted earlier, living conditions in the West were naturally hyperbolic; the popular notion of a condor's wingspan — 14 feet — was half again greater than the reality. The "conquest" of any such enormous animal was a settler's psychological security blanket. As Carroll DeWitt Scott wrote: "Men who dared not meet a grizzly could kill a condor and boast of it the rest of their lives."

It wasn't until the 1930s, after the frontier had been thoroughly domesticated, that condors began to receive real protection. In 1933 the U.S. Forest Service announced plans for a road through Sisquoc Canyon, the center of condor activity in Los Padres National Forest; Robert O. Easton, a militant conservationist who managed the Sisquoc Ranch, objected and was backed by the Audubon Society. Four years later, 1,200 acres surrounding Sisquoc Falls were declared a condor sanctuary, prohibiting public entry except by permit. The bird began to receive national notice, and in the late forties a Condor Advisory Committee was created, as was the 35,000-acre Sespe Wildlife Sanctuary, serving condors (which fly and forage over a much wider range) mainly as a nesting area. In 1950 the San Diego Zoo was actually granted permission to capture condors and breed them in captivity, but in two years not a single condor took the bait; the permit was ultimately revoked by the state legislature, owing largely to the lobbying efforts of Ian McMillan and the Audubon Society, who held that captures might harm the wild flock and, moreover, that the purpose of conservation was the preservation of animals in the wild.

In 1951 the Sespe sanctuary was enlarged to 53,000 acres, chiefly because of concern stimulated by the findings of Carl Koford, a zoologist from the University of California at Berkeley. During the first half of the twentieth century, a predictable difference in orientation existed among American zoologists; while professors at eastern universities were performing anatomic, taxonomic, and embryological studies in laboratories and museums, their western counterparts were likely to be found camping out in the mountains or the desert, watching birds, snakes, rodents, and insects. U.C. Berkeley was a cynosure in this latter galaxy of field biology — a distinction due mainly to the presence of Joseph Grinnell, the first director of its Museum of Vertebrate Zoology.

The son of a government physician (and a distant cousin of George Bird Grinnell, the founder of the Audubon Society), Joseph spent his early childhood in Oklahoma on an Indian reservation, where he was a favorite of Chief Red Cloud; the esteemed Oglala warrior later dictated letters to him as "my little friend Joe." When he was seven years old the family moved to Pasadena, where Mrs. Grinnell, a health food enthusiast, soon gained notoriety by riding a float in the Rose Bowl parade, milking a goat. Joseph graduated from high school at the age of sixteen and promptly collected and classified 158 species of birds within an 8-mile radius of Pasadena. At nineteen he traveled to Alaska, where he performed his avian studies from Indian canoes along the coast. On one trip he was stranded overnight without food or blankets on St. Lazaria Island, 20 miles out to sea; he spent the night analyzing the behavior of petrels. John Muir was among those who inspected his bird collection that summer.

Grinnell published twenty-one scientific papers by the

time he was twenty-one years old; when he died in 1939, the number had reached 554. Alertness encouraged in the company of Indians served him throughout his biological career. One time, leading a group of naturalists in the Mojave Desert, Grinnell correctly determined that kangaroo rats were breeding, although the party hadn't yet sighted any; he had seen the marks of their scrotal sacs in the sand. As a teacher he was tyrannical, insisting that his students duplicate his own uncompromising research methods. If a pupil took any short cuts in arranging and marking specimens, Grinnell would communicate his disapproval by sweeping the student's work onto the floor. His ethics were such that he wouldn't use a university lantern for a field trip that was not university business; nor would he allow students to write personal letters on U.C. typewriters. He founded a system of field notes — binding and cataloguing them for later reference — which is now used by research biologists throughout the world. For thirty-four years he served as editor of *The Condor*, the journal of the Cooper Ornithological Society, in which capacity he functioned as an enemy of ambiguity in manuscripts. One of his students opined that Grinnell "scorned language that was not exact, scientifically accurate and colorless." Yet his originality and humor were apparent in such flourishes as this inclusion of man in a recent mammal fauna of California:

> *Homo sapiens* sapiens Linnaeus. Caucasian . . . non-native, but now thoroughly established and spreading and increasing, chiefly by immigration, at an amazing rate. First came, as voluntary pioneers, in year 1769, settling in a few coastal localities. Increased but slowly until about 1850 when great numbers arrived from many parts of the world. Disposition aggressive and tendencies destructive, especially of natural habitats, as a result of which much of native mammal life, including the endemic race of man (*H. s. americanus*), has

been reduced. . . . Altitudinally, *H. s. sapiens* ranges from 250 feet below sea level (as around Salton Sea) up to 14,000 feet above sea level (on highest peaks, sporadically in summer).

Grinnell was so enamored of California as a bioregion that, on field trips to the hinterlands, he would make a great show of turning the car around at the state line in order to avoid entering alien territory. In an early paper, he described the Colorado River's effect as a barrier to different mammals occupying near-identical desert habitats on either side of it; by some accounts, he was the first biologist to advance the theory that no two species can occupy the same ecological niche and still be different species. He was precocious in seeing the interplay between geography, ecology, and evolution, and hence in advancing the cause of conservation. In his later years, he spoke out increasingly against government programs and poisons, losing personal friends and reaping public abuse in the bargain. As early as 1914 he wrote: "Our successors will not approve of our thoughtlessness in completely destroying the California condor any less than we deplore the wanton destruction of the great auk by our ancestors."

Grinnell was succeeded as editor of *The Condor* and director of the Museum of Vertebrate Zoology by Alden Miller, whose father, Loye, had analyzed condor fossils found at the La Brea tar pits. The son ultimately chose to pursue the previously unexplored paleontology of songbirds. Before he could talk, Alden had listened to his mother playing the Pastorale Symphony on the piano and intervened when she strayed from the music as written by Beethoven and memorized by himself. While at Berkeley, he was a soloist in the First Congregational Church of Oakland; he had a beautiful voice that also enabled him to imitate the objects of his studies. Miller and Grinnell used to escape the tedium of Charter

Day ceremonies at U.C. by keeping competitive lists of the birds that they saw or heard in the university's outdoor amphitheater. Grinnell taught Miller to keep meticulous records and to look for reasons behind superficial data, and Miller's best work makes broad biotic associations in its analysis of the distribution and behavior of animals. In his 1951 paper "Analysis of the Distribution of the Birds of California," Miller identified geographic causes — climatic variation, plant diversity, land barriers, and so forth — for differences in the habits and appearance of various species, an achievement made possible by the firsthand knowledge he gained while collecting samples himself. On field trips, when Miller heard the song of a bird that he sought, he would crawl through thickets of thorns to get at it; in his lifetime he collected more than twelve thousand specimens in the western United States, British Columbia, Central and South America, Australia, and New Guinea.

"Alden Miller was as keen a scientist as I ever saw," says Eben. "With him there were no shades of gray — either something was right, or it was wrong. He was a pillar of integrity. One time he was down here in San Juan Creek collecting plants; some of his students drew straws, and one asked if they could borrow his car to go to a bar in Shandon. He explained to them, not why he wouldn't loan them the car, but why it was wrong that they should conceive that he *might*. He displayed their stupidity, and after that they knew not to try and take advantage of him. They'd cuss him, by George, but ten years later they were proud to have been his students. There are no more of those guys left who'll have their students hating them."

Four fifths of the students who received their Ph.D.'s under Miller were ornithologists. When the Audubon Society offered a fellowship for condor research in 1939, the student whom Miller and Grinnell chose for the job was Carl Koford, a mammalogist. Koford had grown up on a ranch in the San Joaquin Valley and had been trained in forestry and veterinary medicine before he pursued his doctorate in wildlife biology. U.C. zoology students learned their field biology at the Hastings Natural History Reservation in Carmel Valley, where they were made to sit still with a pair of binoculars and a notepad, sizing up the behavior of some species; Koford, somewhat antisocial by nature, sat in a tree watching ground squirrels at Hastings for forty-two consecutive days. As Miller later wrote, he "early appealed to the late Joseph Grinnell and me as a person equipped with the perseverance, ruggedness, and natural instincts for observation which the field study of the California condor absolutely required."

Koford's Audubon fellowship consisted of $1,500 a year for three years. (Sound biological studies take a minimum of three years: one to establish basic data, another to see how those data change, and a third to determine whether the changes represent a pattern.) In March of 1939, Koford took a bus to Pasadena and presented himself to John Pemberton, a geologist and amateur ornithologist who had filmed condors in the wild. Pemberton drove Koford into the Ventura Mountains and left him there with a box of groceries. Over the next two years (he joined the navy in 1941, resuming his research when the war ended), Koford hiked, climbed, and backpacked through, up, and over the canyons, cliffs, and chaparral-covered slopes of condor country. At night, he slept in caves. He said that it "wasn't really bad country because there was water in the potholes." He would spend weeks watching a single roost, sometimes seeing condors for only a few minutes in the course of an entire day. He took 3,500 pages of notes. His meticulousness as an observer is evident in entries such as the following:

The pre-roosting schedule of an especially inactive adult one mild day in August was as follows: 12:05 P.M. alighted in tree. 1:20, flew 100 yards to another tree. 1:45, climbed to higher branch. 2:50, turned around. 3:59, sat. 4:10, stood. 4:12, sat. 4:30, stood, sunned. 4:39, sat. 5:08, stood, sunned. 5:23, sat. 5:25, tucked head in. 6:00, no change.

Among other things, Koford found that condors blinked every two to five seconds; that they yawned just before taking off; that they were often stimulated to fly by the sight of other condors soaring; that they sometimes found food by co-operative effort; that they could survive for several days without feeding; that they habitually pecked and bit at inedible objects; that they preferred the carcasses of deer and calves to those of sheep and heifers but favored the latter over horses and mules; that they ate the eyes, tongue, and anus of a carcass first; that they deferred to golden eagles at carcasses but were dominant over turkey vultures and ravens; and that, if undisturbed, they rarely neglected to feed their young for more than a day. Through a variety of census techniques — counting the birds from single stations, recording simultaneous counts from different stations, and compiling composite counts from observations spaced a few days apart — Koford estimated the total condor population at about sixty.

Fifteen years after Koford's study, Audubon and the National Geographic Society commissioned a new survey of the condor population. Their aim was to assess food supply, reproductive success, range use, and human impact, and compare them with the conditions described by Koford. When Alden Miller was asked for the names of people who might help conduct the new survey, he suggested two that had been instrumental in Koford's original research: Eben and Ian McMillan.

Their study — "The Current Status and Welfare of the California Condor" (Research Report Number Six of the

National Audubon Society) — took place between February of 1963 and August of 1965. Compared with today's radio-telemetry work, the McMillans' methods were primitive (as they still believe biological research should be). Essentially, they spent a lot of time on foot and on horseback and talked to a lot of ranchers to find out where condors were nesting and feeding. They found that most people, upon being questioned, didn't really know what a condor was; one rancher insisted that he had seen a California condor swimming in a lake in Utah. One day Ian got a call saying that forty condors were on a sheep carcass on the east side of the San Joaquin Valley; when he got there he found forty turkey vultures. Even the "condor warden" in the Sespe sanctuary mistook a turkey vulture a hundred yards away for a condor. (The McMillans also discovered that this warden was conducting tours into the off-limits area for people who wanted to look at condors, and was employed part time selling off-road motorcycles for a man who held a grazing permit in the sanctuary.)

Duplicating Koford's methods, Miller and the McMillans concluded that about forty condors were still alive. In other words, in the fifteen years since the previous survey, the population had decreased by one third. It appeared, however, that about a third of the existing birds were juveniles — so reproduction was not the condor's problem. On the contrary, for a species with so youthful a population to be declining so rapidly, a lot of condors had to be getting killed after they left the nest.

Eben and Ian found very few official records of condor deaths; even government rangers had neglected to file reports when condors were known to have died. Still, some mortality factors were obvious. In four years, the McMillans received nine reports of condor shootings; they frequently had offers to shoot condors from people who misunderstood the purpose of their study and, moreover, were unaware that condors, eagles, hawks, and vultures were all protected by law. Eben witnessed one shooting himself — he was talking to the foreman of a squirrel-poisoning crew when two condors came flying over, and he "heard a whack" as one of the crew members fired his rifle. One of the condors, apparently hit, went zigzagging away down a canyon. Eben spent the next day in an airplane trying, unsuccessfully, to find the wounded bird. He turned in the gunman, who admitted in court to having shot at a "buzzard" (also illegal). According to Eben, "The judge turned the guy loose and said, 'You know, he might not have hit that condor. A lot of times a hawk'll flap kind of funny when you shoot at it.' That was evidence that the judge had been shooting at them himself." (To this day, only one person has ever been successfully prosecuted for shooting a condor.)

Another mortality factor was poison. "I doubt that any other region in the world has seen poison used so extensively, so effectively, or with so much ingenuity as in the range of the California condor," Ian wrote in *Man and the California Condor*. "First it was used as a means of killing whatever animals might prey on sheep; later it was used to kill rodents and in some cases birds; and finally in new forms, such as insecticides and herbicides." In the fifties, 150,000 acres along the west side of the San Joaquin Valley were sprayed annually with DDT, and condor eggshells collected during that period were found to be 30 percent thinner than normal. The earlier replacement of the native grasslands with weedy annuals had been accompanied by an infestation of ground squirrels, and San Luis Obispo County ranchers organized poisoning teams, spreading strychnine-treated grain from wagons. "The effect was devastating," Ian wrote. "In 1964 it was possible to drive for hours across San Luis Obispo County without seeing a ground squirrel where the species had been extremely abundant in former years."

Eventually strychnine was outlawed and replaced by thallium sulfate, which was replaced in turn by sodium fluoroacetate — the infamous Compound 1080. Compound 1080 is a synthetic derivative that blocks the body's citric acid ("Krebs") cycle, leading to cell death; it has been described as a supertoxin — one teaspoon is capable of killing 100 adult human beings, and an ounce can eliminate 100,000 squirrels. Colorless and odorless, 1080 doesn't break down in the carcasses of animals that die from it, so it can also be ingested by a scavenger that feeds on a poisoned rodent. Canids — coyotes, wolves, foxes, and dogs — are most susceptible, but when 1080 was in widespread use, it was also found to kill badgers, bobcats, weasels, bears, skunks, ravens, pine martens, eagles, hawks, falcons, and owls.

In October of 1974, nearly three hundred San Luis Obispo County ranches, totaling 653,309 acres, received an aerial shower of 148,715 pounds of grain treated with 1080. In 1966, Ian had found five different species of birds dead under one tree; the area had recently received an aerial application of 1080, and some of the grain baits were still in the birds' crops. Of six condor corpses that the McMillans found between 1960 and 1964, three were near Granite Station in Kern County, where 1080 was being used to poison coyotes. None of the carcasses showed any evidence of external injury. Eben sent one carcass to the U.C. Museum of Vertebrate Zoology, where it was put into a case with dermestid beetle larvae to clean it. Within minutes, the beetles died. No chemical evidence of 1080 was ever found in the tissues of the carcass, rendering the matter inconclusive as far as proof of poisoning was concerned. However, seventeen years later, the U.S. Fish and Wildlife Service inadvertently discovered that 1080 — sodium fluoroacetate — is metabolized into sodium fluoro*citrate* upon being ingested. So there had never been a way of determining chemically whether 1080 had caused the death of a scavenger that had eaten poisoned rodents.

During their study, Eben and Ian uncovered a 1950 report of three condors that had been poisoned by a coyote carcass; one of the birds had died, and chemical analysis showed strychnine in its stomach tissue. The government trapper who put out the carcass told Ian that there had been "great apprehension within the control agency lest information about the poisoned condors spread, and there had been a firm understanding that the matter must remain confidential." Koford, then engaged in his own condor research, had never heard anything about it. Even after the McMillans reported the incident, the Federal Bureau of Sport Fisheries and Wildlife said in its July 1965 Management and Research Plan for the condor: "There seems to be no positive proof that coyote and rodent poisoning programs in the range of the condor have contributed to its decline."

On returning from a research project in Puerto Rico in 1967, Carl Koford criticized the contentions of Sanford Wilbur — then head research biologist for the Condor Recovery Program — that the birds were suffering from problems of food supply and reproduction. Koford, who found that for a hundred years published accounts had attributed condor deaths to poisoned carcasses, offered to conduct a new two-year study of poison's effect on condors. His proposal was turned down by both the Audubon Society and the Fish and Wildlife Service. Roland Clement, Audubon's representative on the Condor Advisory Committee, called Koford's recommendations "irrelevant to our task." Wilbur described the McMillans' warnings about 1080 as "purely and poorly inferential"; in 1977 he wrote: "The problem, if one exists, is almost certainly (note that I said *almost* certainly) not the result of a specific pesticide operation but of a lot of pesticide in the environment generally. Unless a specific source of contamination is found, we can do nothing more than acknowledge the problem and plan around it as best we can. This is what we are doing with our captive-propagation proposal."

In their 1965 report, the McMillans and Alden Miller had recommended that the use of poisoned grain be reduced and poisoning programs timed so as to minimize their impact on condor feeding cycles. They had also recommended specific poison studies on turkey vultures, which are much more numerous than condors but inhabit the same range. They had advised education of hunters and greater enforcement of shooting laws, and they had urged that the shooting of condors be declared a felony. None of these recommendations was ever implemented. Compound 1080 — banned for use on federal land during the administration of Richard Nixon — was made legal again in 1985.

Following his work with condors, Carl Koford went on to study mountain lions in California, spotted cats in Latin America, prairie dogs in Colorado, rhesus monkeys in Puerto Rico, and vicuñas in Peru (this last project represents some of the earliest work done on territoriality in mammals). Throughout his career he resisted specialization, saying that his work with birds informed his work with mammals and vice versa. Although he had an office at U.C. Berkeley, Koford never became a member of any faculty; he preferred to devote himself to pure research, preferably outdoors.

"Koford was an extraordinarily self-sufficient and indefatigable observer," A. Starker Leopold, the renowned wildlife ecologist, told me before his own death in 1983. "If there was something he needed to know, he'd fill his pockets with cheese and prunes and be gone for three days, and by God he'd find out." To the last, Koford was an old-fashioned field man of the sort that traditionally emerged under Grinnell's and Miller's tutelage, employing notebook and binoculars in an environment increasingly characterized by radio collars and computers. So it perhaps comes as no surprise that, to his dying day in 1979, Koford opposed the captive breeding of condors. He thought that human interference couldn't help but disturb nesting; he doubted that condors raised in zoos could survive if released, and he worried that they might even introduce zoo diseases into the wild population. He also pointed out that removing one condor from the wild would also remove all of that condor's progeny for the thirty to forty years of its lifetime. "A condor in a cage is uninspiring, pitiful, and ugly to one who has seen them soaring over the mountains," Koford wrote. "If we cannot preserve condors in the wild through understanding their environmental relations, we have already lost the battle and may be no more successful in preserving mankind."

"Koford was a very unusual fella," Eben told me one night at dinner. He was sitting the way he normally does after a meal, his sinewy arms braced against those of the chair, his clear blue eyes gazing out the window at the late spring landscape as he transported himself back in time. "He had a very peculiar sense of humor — he might break out laughing and be the only one. One time he went hunting with us up on Castle Mountain. Ian's wife, May, had made a chocolate cake for us in a biscuit pan and after dinner we all took a piece. Then Ike said, 'Have another piece of cake, Carl.' We didn't think about it anymore, but after a while we became conscious of this scraping sound. It was Koford scratching the bottom of the pan. He'd eaten the whole cake — he'd been out on one of his starvation routes right before this hunting trip.

"I don't think I ever saw Koford wearing a coat, even right out in the snow. He was always practicing self-discipline; it would have been pretty near impossible to sell him something he didn't need. Koford was a totally objective person — he never joked, never said anything he didn't mean, never went out on a limb. In other words he was a scientist, and it carried over into his personal affairs. He was analyzing things twenty-four hours a day. If the wind came up in the afternoon, he'd ask if it happened all the time. He was never off guard.

"Those condors got to know Koford. They could probably recognize him ten miles away. He himself had very keen eyes, phenomenal eyes. He was sort of a mechanical person — he had no human weaknesses. His integrity was untouchable, which made him unique in a society where integrity has lost its meaning. I'd like to think that he considered Ian and me among his closest, if not friends, then associates."

After dinner, I climbed the hill behind Eben's corral. The sun was setting, and hundreds of rimlit hillocks, dotted with black oaks like leopard spots, were swarming in the west. Beyond them the blue Santa Lucias were topped with a white tissue of coastal fog. In the northeast was the ragged crest of the Diablo Mountains; in the east, the undulant drainage along the San Andreas Fault. There was a leaden lilac thickening in the eastern sky and, below it, a golden hill of foxtail grass with brown and black cattle moving across it. A dark fence line descended the glowing haunch of hill.

Following instructions from Eben, I positioned myself at a point from which a telephone pole directly to the east seemed to stand just to the left of a bare, conical hill on the horizon. From there I moved down until I had lined myself up with the fence, then turned around and climbed the hill. After pacing off thirty-two steps, I looked down and saw a stone on the ground, very near the highest point on Eben's property. Its presence was probably evidence that Koford considered Eben and Ian among his closest associates. This solitary, unmarked rock with a commanding view of condor country was Carl Koford's gravestone.

In THE MORNING a starling crashes into the dining room window, apparently intending to join us for breakfast. "I'm gonna have to get my gun," says Eben. "I see five, six, seven, eight, nine starlings out there. Tomorrow there'll be ninety. Then there'll be nine hundred. If we went away for three days, they'd move in and paint the house." The birds are the bane of Eben's existence. "Most pests have *some* beneficial effect," he says, "and starlings eat a lot of insects. But mostly they're just a complete nuisance."

Starlings — whose overall relationship with human beings is indicated by the species' scientific name, *Sturnus vulgaris* — have never been terribly popular. In 1932, E. R. Kalmbach described the attitude of citizens in Washington, D.C., toward the bird: "Here the shopper and shop-owner; the pedestrian and autoist; the bird hater and even bird lover periodically join the chorus of damnation. Even the staid ranks of profound ornithologists have echoed the song of lament." The reason for this refrain, as Walter E. Howard put it in the *Bulletin of the California Department of Agriculture* in 1959, is quite simply that "most of the starling's activities are irritating to man." *Sturnus vulgaris* doesn't go in for singing, except to imitate other birds. He does destroy injurious insects, but he also devours beneficial ones. In general, he eats whatever's handy — seeds, corn, pears, figs, olives, cherries, berries, and grapes (which are consumed crudely, with uneaten bunches bruised and battered to the ground). Gathering around cattle lots in winter when food is scarce, starlings consume huge quantities of livestock feed and spread disease among cattle through their feces. Combative by nature, they threaten the survival of more mild-mannered hole-nesting birds such as wrens, bluebirds, swallows, and woodpeckers; they have been known to kill downy woodpecker young in the nest and even to prevent sparrow hawks from nesting. Congregating in huge flocks in late winter and early spring, starlings can scour a landscape of all available food just before the northward migration of other species.

This flocking habit is probably the starling's trait that most exasperates man. As fledglings the birds begin gathering in small groups, which continue to merge until all the starlings in an area have formed one vast flock, sometimes numbering in the millions. In the summer they collect in trees in such numbers that they can break major limbs or kill them with their accumulated droppings; in cold weather they move to buildings, where their nests create a fire hazard, their excrement an eyesore, and their uncultured cacophony a public nuisance. In 1926, the *Western Morning News and Mercury* in Plymouth, England, reported that "bands of inhabitants have stood in the woods and created all manner of noises to frighten the [starlings] away, but they return at dark, and then nothing will keep them out. Thousands of them have been shot, but still many more thousands come."

The starling is native to Eurasia, but it was purposefully introduced to the United States at the turn of the century. At the time — such a fervid one for the study of natural history in America — acclimatization societies existed across the country for the purpose of "improving" the native avifauna by importing exotic bird species. One Eugene Scheifflin, an eccentric druggist in New York City, voluntarily shouldered the task of introducing every bird mentioned in Shake-speare's works. In *Henry IV, Part I,* when the king refuses to ransom Mortimer and forbids any discussion of him, Hot-spur proclaims that he'll "have a starling shall be taught to speak nothing but 'Mortimer,' and give it him." So Scheifflin turned a hundred starlings loose in Central Park.

Starlings are highly prolific and adaptable. Within a year of Scheifflin's release, the birds were nesting — appropriately enough — under the eaves of the American Museum of Natural History. By 1910 their descendants had emigrated to Philadelphia; by 1912, Washington, D.C.; by 1913, Boston. The uncouth critters cut a swath across New York State by way of the Mohawk Valley and made Ohio theirs in 1916. In 1919 they crossed the Canadian border and demanded drinks in St. Catharines, Ontario. The year before that, following a severe northeast storm, a solitary starling was sighted near Montgomery, Alabama; two years later he had become a large flock. In the winter of 1920–21, five hundred starlings spent two months near Nashville, making country music with cowbirds.

Illinois succumbed in 1922, Wisconsin in 1923. In 1925, May Thatcher Cooke surmised: "How much [the starling] will extend its range on to the plains is a question, for it seems hardly probable that it will find much territory there suitable to its requirements." Texas, 1926. Oklahoma, 1929. Nebraska, 1930. South Dakota, 1933. Colorado, 1938. In

1942, a flock of forty starlings was reported near Tule Lake, California; within fifteen years there were 50,000 of them in the San Joaquin Valley, where the mild climate, endless acres of irrigated pasture, and vast fields of one-cereal crops presented a veritable paradise. Today the starling is probably the most common bird in California, where the species annually causes more than $12 million of agricultural damage.

"Exotics have the advantage in having lived with man," says Eben. "Starlings don't seem to associate us with any danger at all. Native animals will keep their distance and never really do any harm; orioles might give you a problem with figs, but not really that bad. But if you let starlings come in when the olives are ripe, pretty soon you'll have two thousand birds in one tree.

"There hasn't been a starling camped out on this place overnight in twenty years that I know of. The problem is, when I shoot them, I scare off the blackbirds too. And the blackbird is a nice bird, one you want to keep around. Starlings aren't really a *bad* bird; they're an interesting, pugnacious thing. The other day I saw one attack a red-winged blackbird with no provocation whatsoever. My fight with them is that they run off all the desirable birds — birds I prefer."

A somewhat milder botanical version of starlings — and one that illustrates even better the role played by *Homo sapiens* when it comes to the establishment of exotic species — is offered by eucalyptus, the Australian tree that for many people now fairly epitomizes the California landscape. Eucalyptus (the name derives from the Greek *eu*, "well," and *kaluptos*, "covered") first became known to the West in 1770, thanks to Captain James Cook and his sidekick, the botanist Sir Joseph Banks, who quickly discovered that eucalypts had many remarkable properties. To begin with, the trees are pretty — they bend and rustle in the wind, exuding an agreeable smell; the drooping, shaggy leaves range from blue- to gray-green, the long ribbons of bark from white to dark pink. Their wood is hard enough to be used in furniture; the karri (*Eucalyptus diversicolor*) and tuart (*E. gomphocephala*) varieties are so strong that they've replaced steel in railroad tracks, and the jarrah (*E. marginata*) has lasted for fifty years in wharf pilings and fence posts. The mountain ash (*E. regnans*) is the tallest broad-leafed tree in existence; in the mountains of Victoria and Tasmania it grows up to 300 feet (second in height only to California's sequoias). The blue gum (*E. globulus*) is reputed to be the world's *fastest*-growing tree: from seed, it can reach a height of 35 feet in fifteen months. Eucalypts are gluttons for moisture, but, interestingly, they're also drought-resistant; even though they're evergreen, they shed leaves during dry weather to conserve water.

After Cook's voyage, eucalypts were transplanted to Mauritius, the Mediterranean, India, South Africa, and North America. They did even better abroad than in Australia, where they tend to be limited partly by the koala (which feeds upon them exclusively) and partly by leaf-eating insects that have evolved with the more than six hundred eucalyptus species that exist there. Eucalypts are spectacularly adaptable — they'll grow almost anywhere that the winters aren't too severe, which of course constitutes strong candidacy for citizenship in California. Like a great many other exotic organisms, they first came to the West Coast in the Gold Rush era, when it took about as long to reach San Francisco from Sydney as it did from Boston or New York. At first the trees were sold at exorbitant prices as luxury items and ornamentals, but they grew so quickly that prices soon dropped and newspapers and farm journals began publishing advice on their care. They were found to be first-rate sources of shade and firewood, and their oil was said to relieve rheumatism and gout. In southern California, where the Santa Ana winds had destroyed the state's first citrus orchards, the fast-growing blue gums were planted to protect the fruit from the wind (today there are still thousands of miles of eucalyptus windbreaks in California's agricultural valleys). Near Bakersfield, the trees actually got rid of malaria by draining whole areas of standing water and thus eliminating mosquito habitat.

By the 1880s the eucalyptus was the most popular plantation tree in California. In 1904 an alarm was sounded to the effect that America's hardwood supply had only twenty years to go, and the federal government responded by publishing the growth records of eucalypts in California; over the next eight years, 50,000 acres of row-on-row eucalyptus forests were planted. On Arbor Days, bunches of eucalyptus seedlings were distributed to San Francisco schoolchildren. Jack London planted 100,000 of them on Sonoma Mountain. Somebody else planted 170,000 for firewood in the East Bay hills, near Hayward. Speculators bought land for $15 an acre, purchased eucalyptus seedlings for $5 per thousand, planted the trees, and sold the land for $250 an acre — claiming that in ten years the timber would be worth ten times as much. By 1910, at least a hundred companies in California and the Southwest were dealing in eucalyptus commodities: timber, land, seed, oil, or simply information. An ad placed by the Eucalyptus Timber Company of Kansas City read:

A Problem in Finance

If Productive Land Equals Safety, and Growing Hardwood Timber Equals Large Profits, what will the Combination of the Two Equal?

Answer: Eucalyptus

A judicious investment in Eucalyptus Timber will make you more money than can be made on the best farm land.

No Work

Put your surplus into Eucalyptus and after ten years you can live on the income the rest of your life and when you are gone your children and your children's children will perpetually reap the same

Large Profits
If you could be convinced that these statements are true, you would not hesitate one day, but would send us your money by telegraph. . . .

Four fifths of the eucalyptus timber plantings were of the blue gum variety, which attains in fifteen years the volume that less prolific hardwoods yield in fifty or seventy-five. It was soon discovered, however, that timber from such young trees lacked the quality of more mature lumber. Frank Havens, the president of the People's Water Company of Berkeley, spent a quarter of a million dollars planting eucalyptus in the Oakland hills; he commissioned a study which found that trees less than 2½ feet in diameter could not be made into decent lumber — high-quality eucalyptus apparently required growth of thirty years or more. As a matter of fact, in Australia the blue gum was not even considered a timber tree — its miraculous qualities render it unsuitable for lumber. For example, the reason that *E. globulus* can bend as much as forty-five degrees in the wind is that its tensile strength is three times its compression strength; when the tree is felled, these forces relinquish their equilibrium and the wood develops checks in the pith, which run out radially and expand over time. The tree's remarkable ability to store moisture corresponds to an equally remarkable tendency to shrink as soon as it begins to dry out, resulting in the evaporation of as much as 15 percent of its volume. The best blue gum wood originates on the hillsides of Tasmania, which receive thirty to fifty inches of rainfall annually — these trees sometimes yield perfectly clear grained, 60-foot logs. In the drier California climate, *globulus* lumber possesses a profusion of dead knots.

The upshot of America's eucalyptus timber craze was 50,000 acres of lumber so deformed as to be unusable; the boom expired even before its initial ten-year payoff period was up, resulting in millions of dollars of losses by investors all over the country. The unharvested *trees* remained, however, growing as fast and thick as expected. When you chop a eucalyptus down, the stump sends out shoots, each of which becomes a new trunk. Pretty soon you can't see the forest for the trees — especially if the former was oak, originally the dominant woodland at California's lower elevations. Where they fall, the shed leaves and bark of the eucalyptus — so beautiful to look at and so full of oil — inspire alkaline reactions in the soil, suppressing the growth of many native plants (except poison oak, which thrives). Though they don't really constitute the "biological desert" that they were termed in the backlash following the timber fiasco, California's eucalyptus groves support a poorer biota — that is to say, one less diverse — than existed before their arrival. (For one thing, their inhospitability to native insects results in a weaker concentration of birds.) Given their first-rate fuel potential and tremendous concentration of fallen detritus — as much as eighty tons per acre — they also constitute a major fire hazard from July through October, when California brush fires annually make nationwide news. Eucalyptus oil evaporates upon being heated, creating an explosive atmosphere that can propel fireballs over several miles. In 1922 a frost killed a sizable batch of eucalyptus in the Berkeley hills, and the following year a fire that began there burned down a third of the city.

A few years ago, Eben planted a stand of red gum eucalyptus on his ranch for firewood. He says they grow fast, but claims they don't spread: "When you cut one down it sends out new shoots, but no new trees. I don't think any organism should be considered feral as long as it can't move from where it is. They say that, in ten years' time, each tree'll give you a cord of wood." He was seventy-five when he planted the trees; nevertheless, he doesn't refrain from beginning such projects.

"Sometimes I overhear somebody referring to me as an old man," Eben says. "Usually, the person saying it is somebody I can outrun. I remember when I was a kid — somebody who was seventy-five was just about ready for the junkyard. I suppose I'll degenerate someday, but I keep surprising myself. A lot of this can be psychological."

When Eben gets up in the morning, he walks on his tiptoes for five minutes; then he bends over with his head between his knees; then he does sit-ups in slow motion and rolls on his back in the fetal position; still on his back, he makes fifteen circles with his legs in the air without letting them touch the ground; stretches one leg at a time with the other one pulled up to his chest; does ten knee bends on one leg with the other one extended behind him; does twelve push-ups; lets the chickens out; then does fifteen chin-ups on a board nailed to a tree. His biceps protrude from his arms in the manner of mammals swallowed by snakes. As a result of a couple of horseback accidents, Eben's left leg contains no kneecap, but he never sits down while putting on his shoes and socks. "It tones my balance up a bit," he explains. He walks with a limp — at a pace that tends to tire out taggers-along.

In hot, dry weather — July, August, September — Eben sleeps on the front porch. He has a bed there, with iron headboards and a quilt decorated with ranch scenes: a barn, a scarecrow, a hay wagon. When the nights turn foggy, he sleeps in a room in the back of the house. Often he wakes up in the middle of the night and can't get back to sleep. "One of the troubles I have with sleeping is getting stuck on some train of thought," he says. "I try not to get my mind fixed on any one thing, but it's not that easy. I was always a poor man

for putting problems aside; I might start thinking about nuclear power, or I might lay awake half the night trying to remember somebody's name."

When Eben can't sleep, he reads — usually "heavy material, current philosophy and human problems. I'm a very
poor, slow reader. I read a lot, but — I shouldn't say I read a
lot. I spend a lot of *time* reading." A sample of titles from
Eben's bookshelves includes Armstrong's *Bird Display and Behavior*, Austin's *Land of Little Rain*, Barbour and Davis's *Bats of
America*, Brewer's *Up and Down California*, Coville's *Botany of
Death Valley*, Crompton's *The Spider*, Dale's *Indians of the
Southwest*, Davis's *Let's Eat Right to Keep Fit*, Davis's *Modern
Dog Encyclopedia*, Dawson's four-volume *Birds of California*,
Doig's *This House of Sky*, Eastman and Hunt's *Parrots of Aus-
tralia*, Essig's *Insects of the World: A Checklist*, Franklin's *Autobi-
ography*, Gudde's *California Place Names*, Harrington's *Western
Edible Wild Plants*, Iacopi's *Earthquake Country*, Kjelgard's
Coming of the Mormons, Koford's *California Condor*, two editions
of Leopold's *A Sand County Almanac*, Lorenz's *On Aggression*,
McMillan's *Man and the California Condor*, Motor's *Truck and
Diesel Repair Manual*, Murphy's *Oceanic Birds of South America*,
Robbins, Bellue, and Ball's *Weeds of California*, Rutledge's
Spanish Dictionary, Thomas's *Lives of a Cell*, Thomas's *Conser-
vation of Ground Water*, Todd's *Stars and Telescopes*, Van
Tramp's *Prairie and Rocky Mountain Adventures, or: Life in the
West*, Wood and Fyfe's *Art of Falconry of Frederick II*, a twelve-
volume history of Canada, the botany and ornithology vol-
umes of the Geological Survey of California, records of the
North American Wildlife Conference from 1932 to 1965,
twenty-three volumes of the U.S. Government's yearbooks
on agriculture from 1894 to 1967, and sixty-two volumes of
The Auk dating through 1945 (valued by Eben at $3,000).

There is a conspicuous absence of fiction. "Fiction doesn't
have any information in it," Eben explains. "Would you let

some guy come in your house and tell you lies all day long? Mark Twain wasn't honest; he was an entertainer. He described a coyote as a slinking, fearful, skulky, half-starved cur. Those are *human* terms. In nature, those characteristics have a purpose: they enable the animal to survive in a complex environment. Mark Twain didn't know a damn thing about it. He misled people. I don't have time for that; there are too many things I need to know. I could be reading something constructive."

Every year, Eben rereads *A Sand County Almanac* "sort of the way people read the Bible — so I don't feel like I'm just some nut." When I told him that I do the same thing with *Walden*, he said, "Thoreau was never easy for me. I always had the feeling that he wasn't really part of the environment — it was like he was trying to describe some person he'd met. He had to work at it; he wasn't free." Then, in one of the best descriptions of a soiled kettle that I have ever heard given by a darkened pot, Eben said, "He was a little bit like a preacher."

Eben has to fix the roof. Using a pair of metal shears, he cuts up seven 24- by 23-inch aluminum sheets. He bought three thousand of the sheets from the *San Luis Obispo Telegram Tribune*, where they were once used as stencils for newspaper pages — they're covered with classified ads, headlines about car wrecks, pictures of politicians. Eben wipes each one clean, flattens its edges with a cement trowel, and, using a nail and a framing square, divides the sheet into a grid. With the shears he cuts each sheet into six rectangles and finally carries a stack of forty-two onto the roof.

The house posts holding up the roof are adorned with antlers of elk and antelope, gigantic pine cones and horseshoes, an old Spanish bit, a curry comb, a railroad spike, an ox shoe, a wagon wrench, and a coyote trap hanging from a chain. On the ground is an Indian acorn-grinding rock and a cattle brand that once belonged to George Hearst (father of William Randolph). "I found it in a ditch on the Hearst Ranch," Eben says. "I picked up the trap there, too. Hearst didn't want any animals killed — he made his Chinaman gardener trap mice and take them far enough away from the house that they wouldn't come back. When I was a kid, everybody always told wild tales about what was going on at the Hearst Castle; supposedly there were senators and movie actors always coming and going, and we heard that if you were caught trespassing, they'd bury you right out in the hills. It was like the den of the Wizard of Oz."

Using a two-foot screwdriver and an iron crowbar, Eben pries up rows of wooden shingles. "The roofers put felt underneath the shingles, but the sun gets between the gaps and rots the felt and it leaks," he says. Performing preventive maintenance, he periodically checks each row for weak spots and poor alignments, yanking the old sheets out with pliers and replacing them with new ones that overlap. The entire roof now has aluminum under its shingles, shining in strips at the bottom of each row. Eben says that sometimes the sheets blow off during storms; he looks out his window, and the governor's face flies past like a ghost.

He spits tobacco juice onto the roof while he works. I notice that he isn't wearing a watch. "I try to keep away from counting time," he says. "It makes things simpler. After a while, you get to where you're fighting a watch — you're always thinking: now it's ten-thirty, now it's eleven-thirty . . . If I have to meet somebody at the mailbox at eleven o'clock, I'll just get there early and wait. My time isn't that important. I can always watch birds."

Descending from the roof, Eben goes to the garden. He begins digging up cabbages with a pitchfork and dropping them onto the ground. "I had a dandy stand of cabbage last winter, and I thought they were really gonna do good. Then they bolted and wouldn't form a head." A black beetle crawls out from under one of the cabbages. Eben unconsciously lifts his heel to let the bug pass. "I'm gonna feed this cabbage to the chickens. Usually I just feed them local barley — weed seed, stems, trash. I buy it for about a cent a pound." From his chickens Eben gets more than two dozen eggs per day. His eggs are to supermarket eggs as whipping cream is to skim milk. "The chickens you get in the store are grown in a hothouse," he explains. "It's not a natural environment for them, and they're flimsy. Ranch-grown chickens are so tough you can't break their bones. I had a friend once who was raising chickens commercially; he came home late one night and let them out to peck around a little, and when he closed up the coop, he didn't realize it but he'd locked a bobcat inside. During the night that bobcat killed ... I can't remember exactly right now, but it seems to me it was about two hundred and forty chickens. Once they get excited and start fluttering around, it's a defensive reaction on the part of the bobcat."

Eben returns the tools to the barn, putting them down among halters and bridles, a couple of saddles, a pair of hip waders, an old lantern, a backpack, and several bags of soap. The soap is made from animal fat and hangs from a rafter so that mice can't eat it. On the wall there's a cardboard hand-lettered sign saying TULE ELK — ONE HALF MILE. There's also a small postcard painting of Yosemite Valley.

"When we were first going to Yosemite in the twenties, you'd meet people there that you knew," says Eben. "There wasn't any advertising like they have in the Valley now, so you learned most things yourself. You could spread out your sleeping bag below where the service station and the government center are today, and you'd hear coyotes, rocks falling, the wind up in the spires; there was good fishing in the Valley, and the scent was just exhilarating. Now you dasn't take a deep breath of air. The Valley is a honky-tonk. My God, you could get run over! I think they ought to make it so that people have to walk in; that used to be the long-range plan, but then somebody asked what the people in wheelchairs would do. Well, what do the people in wheelchairs do about Mount Everest? There shouldn't be special privileges."

In a smaller building downhill from the barn is a chest of drawers exuding the odor of mothballs. It contains Eben's avian collection — swallows, swifts, hawks, starlings, flickers, magpies, warblers, curlews, jays, larks, wrens, finches, gulls, ducks, grebes: more than a hundred feathered skins. Below that building is the McMillans' guest cabin, a shelter that has saved the skins of hundreds of environmentalists. On the knotty-pine interior walls hang pictures of a golden-winged woodpecker and a Carolina turtle dove. The first sight that greets someone waking in the cabin is a window that frames a wheat-planted hillside; one becomes cognizant of it precisely at dawn, when the birds in the trees go off like an alarm. In early afternoon, however, mourning doves exert the opposite effect (if "exert" can be applied to their supremely gentle intonations). Many times, after eating lunch — the big meal of the day at the McMillans' — I have retired to this cabin and, lulled by the sound of the wind in the trees and the rhythmic cooing of the doves, nodded off for an hour or so before addressing afternoon business. The soothing cadence of the doves seems the very essence of calmness; in this pacific place, it becomes the sound of a harmonious kingdom, a tranquil environment, an unperturbed planet. It is, I realized after considerable meditation, the sound of a world at peace.

ONE FOGGY MORNING, I set out walking from Eben's house. The tops of the surrounding hills were obscured in the fog; the entire world was gray and yellow. I climbed half a mile on the Gillis Canyon Road, listening to birds, crickets, and the lowing of an invisible cow. Pretty soon a barbed-wire fence came along; where it crossed the road, there was a cattle guard flanked by white two-by-six gates hung with old tires. Attached to the wire that held the tires were some faded blue and white Pepsi and Budweiser cans. The red had long since been obliterated by the sun.

Beyond the cattle guard the road descended, and hills dove in from both left and right. Fog can dissipate quickly when you cross a ridgeline, and immediately I began to see patches of blue in the sky. By the time I got to the bottom of the hill the fog had cleared completely, lingering only in pinkish clouds on the western horizon toward the coast. The sunlit canyon opened to reveal, of all things, a grove of trees. There were seventy or so, of various species: pepper, cotton-wood, gooseberry, eucalyptus — even some apples and al-monds — and they were full of singing birds. In the middle of the grove was a run-down brown adobe hut. A bunch of black cattle galloped away at my approach, accompanied by a gray and brown white-throated coyote.

I left the road and began climbing a ridge to the south, flushing a barn owl as I passed through the trees. Its flight was steady and impressive, powered and regulated by its broad beating wings. (Eben thinks that barn owls fly more effortlessly than any other bird, and says that aside from hummingbirds and Say's phoebes, they're the only birds that can fly straight *up*.) When I got to the top of the ridge, I looked out at land stretching clear to the Coast Range. The country had been sculpted by eons of wind, and the hills vi-brated with optical effects. Some looked almost human — nude torsos with furrows and orifices, lying on top of one an-other in the sun. Oddly, the arid landscape seemed to suggest water. It was oceanic in feeling and in scope — forceful, diz-zying, gigantic.

On the other side of the ridge was another yellow valley with brown outbuildings. Watched on all sides — by cattle and a circling redtailed hawk — I descended a rutted ranch road to the valley floor, where I saw a beige pickup moving at the almost imperceptible pace that characterizes ranch supervision. Inside the truck, wearing a sweat-stained gray cowboy hat and a pink western shirt and a flap of skin under his throat that made him look like a Brahma bull, was Ian I. ("Ike") McMillan.

I had met Ian only once, on my first trip to Eben's ranch after the condor hearing, but I knew a fair bit about him. He had been a fellow of the California Academy of Sciences, a member of the board of directors of Defenders of Wildlife, and a commissioner (under Governor Ronald Reagan) for the California Department of Parks and Recreation at a time when it had doubled the acreage of state parks. I had, of course, read his book *Man and the California Condor* and a number of articles he had written for magazines such as *Audubon* and *Defenders*. These ranged from scientific studies like "The Concentration of Band-Tailed Pigeons in Central California in 1949" to discursive essays like "Doing Away with Wildness," an indictment of the captive breeding of whooping cranes. His writing was formal and often indignant, but usually not devoid of humor. Ian was a prodigious letter-writer; in the sixties he had lobbied for the protection of sand dunes, against the development of recreational parks in wilderness areas, against DDT and 1080, against the removal of plant growth from the Salinas River, against the hunting of does during deer season. He had also been the first local person to protest the nuclear power plant at Diablo Canyon, in western San Luis Obispo County; he was arrested there in 1977.

Superficially, Ian appeared to be the activist where Eben was the philosopher. I had heard that he was hardheaded and intolerant where Eben was relatively diplomatic. "Ike is abrupt and blunt and not patient," Starker Leopold had told me. "He has a rather brash approach to conservation issues. He's always challenging somebody — even his best friend. He'll tell anybody off. I admire him for it; I could never do it."

A. Starker Leopold (son of Aldo, the author of *A Sand County Almanac*, the literary cornerstone of modern conservationist philosophy) had first encountered the McMillans in the late 1940s, when he came to Berkeley to serve as Alden Miller's assistant. "Miller told me there were two fellas I had to meet," Leopold said. "I went down there to talk to Ike about managing quail; he'd already been thinking about it, and pretty soon he was so far ahead of me that he was telling me how to do it. It's very unusual for a rancher with nothing but a simple farm education to have such a deep understanding of ecology. The Fish and Game boys have been going down there for years to see how Ike does things. You can trace ideas that are being implemented now in Nevada and Arizona right back to Ike McMillan."

Ian eventually wrote the foreword to Leopold's book *The California Quail*, in which he called quail the embodiment of "the fat of the land." But Ian had rejected co-authorship of the book when Leopold — along with a great many others — recommended the use of fire as a land management tool.

"There are very few places that *never* burn, like the Olympic peninsula," Leopold told me. "Chaparral used to burn over once every three to five years, either because of lightning or because the Indians would do it. But Ike won't admit that there's any place for fire in any kind of management. I think it's because of his desert background. He has very deep feelings for woody growth — it enrages him to see chaparral burning to get better grazing. He and I agree on damn near everything else, but he wouldn't back off and admit that fire could be a benefit." Before the book was published, Leopold had been a regular at McMillan quail hunts — events of no small political importance in California environmental circles — but after opposing Ian on the fire issue, he was never again invited.

Further illuminating Ian's temperament, Leopold said that Ike had once gotten into a fistfight with another Defenders of Wildlife board member. Eben had told me about a fishing trip on which Ian arrived at a High Sierra lake on horseback and found a forest ranger fishing from a helicopter; Ian absconded with the copter keys, and the ranger had to walk out. "Ike's more apt to follow things through than you or I or the average man," Eben explained. "He's like a bulldog — he just hangs on. If I saw somebody cutting a fence, I'd berate him; but Ike would find out who he worked for. He was feared by a lot of corporations that sustained themselves by taking privileges with the rights of individuals."

Eben referred to Ian as a "perfectionist," a characterization I had gleaned from elements in Ian's book. For example, discussing the identification of condors, Ian had written: "It seems that the only way to be sure of a person's ability to identify condors at a distance is to be in the field with that person and note his identification of birds that could possibly be mistaken for condors. If, using binoculars of about seven power, he distinguishes accurately between a golden eagle and turkey vulture on the wing at a distance of about two miles, and between a redtailed and a Swainson hawk at a mile, he should pass as a dependable condor watcher." While the accurate identification of condors was essential to the McMillans' 1963–65 study, these carefully considered criteria struck me as highly specific and not very flexible.

"I've never stolen anything or cheated a man," Eben said, "but now and then I might've done something like take the wheels off a person's car at Halloween — something you wouldn't want somebody else to do to *you*. But I don't think Ike has ever done anything he thought was wrong."

Ian got out of his truck to greet me. Approaching slowly, he reached behind his belt to pull up his jeans. He walked with his elbows and arms suspended out from his sides, which, together with the fact that he seemed to be balancing precariously on top of his cowboy boots, gave him a rather rickety appearance. When he extended his hand I saw that, like Eben's, it had a gesticulatory deformity: his index finger took a ninety-degree turn at the outermost joint — the result of a childhood accident with a window. Ian had less hair and was bigger than Eben; if Ian were indeed a bull, Eben would be something like a badger. Ian's eyebrows peaked and wafted out from his forehead, and combined with the angle at which he cocked his cowboy hat, they gave him a haughty, discriminating air.

We exchanged pleasantries; I told him what I'd seen on my walk. As we spoke, from the corner of my eye I saw a lizard perched on a post — with its front legs, it was raising and lowering its chest. I asked Ian what the lizard was doing, and he laughed. "Push-ups!" he said. "It's a display. He probably sees another lizard somewhere. It's characteristic of them; it serves as a kind of ego attraction. If you looked at some guy lifting weights, and then got close up and looked at the face of that lizard — why, it'd probably be just about the same look."

The post was part of a fence that enclosed about an acre of Ian's property. Native plants — atriplex and horehound — were growing inside it. There was also a water tank with brush piled on top and a cement dish 15 feet in diameter. These were all part of Ian's semilegendary system of quail preservation. The cement dish caught rainwater during the winter and acted as a reservoir in summer, attracting and sustaining birds all year long. The brush piles served as roosts, as Ian discovered during the forties. Originally his ranch had very few quail on it, but between 1947 and 1949 he increased the population by more than 700 percent. Leopold once climbed a hill and took a picture of the area around Ian's house; later he put the photo under a microscope and counted a thousand quail in one covey.

"A year from now, two thirds of the quail here will be dead," Ian said. "They're all here for the benefit of predators. Quail make food for prairie falcons, snakes, skunks, bobcats. They increase the diversity of the ecosystem."

When we got into his truck, I noticed that Ian's keychain had a picture of a condor on it. "Even more than for the condor, I've been trying to get attention here for the deterioration of land," he said. "Soil conservation now is worse than it was forty years ago." We came to a fence where Ian's ranch bordered his neighbor's. On Ian's side, the range was yellow; on the neighbor's, brown. The grass wasn't terribly tall in either case, but if Ian's was shorn in the style of a 1957 college student, the neighbor's had just joined the Marines. You could see the land's tender, fertile scalp — the topsoil — through the scant growth.

"When those steep hills are plowed and exposed, water runs down and picks up clay and rocks," Ian said. "Pretty soon it's not just water anymore — it's an abrasive substance that cuts and scours." We were now parked alongside the result, a miniature version of the Grand Canyon, running through the middle of Ian's land. "Erosion now is worse than it was in the Dust Bowl days," he said. "There's a natural recovery if you're losing three or four tons of topsoil per acre, but not if you're losing sixty. I've worked for years on an approach to this. I'll show you what we did."

He turned the truck around and drove back down the canyon. I got a glimpse of Ian's house, a low, relatively modern ranch structure set amid oaks, junipers, and pepper trees on a flat spot of ground. Next to it was a corral containing a chestnut horse with one stirrup hooked to its saddle horn. We drove down the dirt road through a lot of low shrubs, rejoining the eroded ravine below the house. Ian stopped the truck and got out. The day had blossomed into a balmy example of California spring — the cottonwoods were bending in the breeze, shimmering and reflecting the sunlight. A big brown and white bull, which had been lying in the dust, got up at our approach.

The gully opened out into a wash. Ian pushed down on the

top strand of a barbed-wire fence that bordered it. "Just steady that for me so I can get over," he said as he hobbled out onto the streambed, a powdery plain pockmarked with puddles and animal tracks. "What's that, a coyote?" he said, glancing at the prints. (He pronounced it "kye-oat.") "Yeah, a big coyote. Sometimes you see bobcat tracks here. Those over there are quail." Among the tracks, twigs of tamarisk, willow, and cottonwood stuck up out of the mud. "Look at that," said Ian. "A little willow. We broke off the twigs to build the fence, and now they're gonna grow. The flood washed it and covered it, and eventually it'll be a thicket. Fantastic. Beautiful!"

Ian said he had built the barbed-wire fence to keep cattle from eating the bushes that sprang up in the topsoil that washed down from his neighbor's ranch. Upstream was an earthen dam serving the same purpose; it was responsible for the shrubs through which we'd driven on our way to the streambed. Ian had written a witty article about all of this. He called it "How to Become a Real Conservationist":

> Get possession of a good acreage of new, rich land, most of which is sharply rolling, and when stripped of all vegetative cover and intensely cultivated is highly vulnerable to erosion. Set up on this property a program of maximum, immediate production and profit. Obtain all government aid and assistance possible. . . . Intensive, modern cropping techniques will result. Normal rainfall, sluicing off the exposed slopes, carrying with it loads of topsoil, will cut deep gorges in the rich bottom lands. Where an especially deep gorge of this kind is cut across a central and most productive part of your ranch, put in a conservation dam. Additional conservation funds will be readily issued. . . . trees and shrubs will spring up in the rich, wet deposits; various species of wildlife will move into this new habitat . . . and people who come to your ranch and see this final development will say that you are a 'Real Conservationist.'

"I did this as an experiment. There was no interest," Ian declared. "Anyway, the work is to keep the topsoil where it belongs — on the slopes. But today everything is oriented to economics; production is the bottom line."

To Ian McMillan, who once blamed the increased shooting of condors on the marksmanship of returning veterans, World War II was a watershed in the deterioration of North America. "After that we changed from a society that just took pleasure in achieving to one that was oriented toward production for profit," he said. "That was when we saw the coming of the bulldozer, of technology and fertilizer. If it weren't for those things, a lot of this land would be out of cultivation." Farmers began plowing steep hillsides during the war, when maximum production was patriotic and wheat was high-priced. (Conservation is actually discouraged by both boom and bust economies. When prices are high, the financial returns for heavy production are invariably higher than for a conservation project on the order of Ian's dam; when prices are low, arid-land ranchers have to use all their available resources just to stay solvent. The tax structure, which assesses land according to its most lucrative potential, also encourages overproduction: if a farmer leaves his land idle in order to replenish it, he still has to pay the same taxes that would result from an opulent crop. If he grazes it — the least remunerative return — the temptation is to run as many cattle on it as he can.)

Ian divides his ranch into sections and rotates them among grazing, farming, and fallowing. On average, he takes a crop of wheat or barley from each section every five or six years. "What I've got in mind is long-range versus short-range production, over a hundred or two hundred years. Most farmers fallow the land every other year, then pour chemical fertilizer on it and get a bumper. But there's no question that the basic fertility of the land is going downhill. Maybe it looks perfect to you, but if you understand the principles involved, you see beyond the immediate to the ultimate; you can almost look at a piece of land and tell how long it'll be before the fella has to move on."

The exhaustion of farmland is as old as agriculture. Man learned to irrigate before he learned to read or write, before he created stable government, before he engaged in extensive trade. But, with few exceptions, he has never maintained a progressive civilization in one place for more than forty to sixty generations. Traditionally, major civilizations have begun on "new" (i.e., previously unexploited) land and flourished for a few centuries as the wildlife was killed, the forests razed, the grasslands denuded. When the land would no longer support the people, they invaded their neighbors; when the limits of conquest were reached, the civilizations fell. So complete was the ruination of the land that today the original "cradles of civilization" — the valleys of the Nile, the Euphrates, and the Indus, in Egypt, Iran, and Pakistan — are populated mainly by peasant farmers and nomadic herdsmen. Poor leadership, political corruption, misguided economics, and that most subjective condition — "moral decay" — usually contributed to the demise, but by far the most important factor has been the availability of raw materials from natural resources. Great civilizations don't decline until their land is depleted.

In this scheme of things, one difference between the United States and the dominant civilizations that have preceded it is that America represents the last major area of "new" land in the world. Another is twentieth-century technology, which has accelerated destructive processes that once required thousands of years. This is why America has already begun to show signs of environmental exhaustion after only three centuries — twelve generations — of civilization. One such sign is the fact that 10 percent of the land in the United States (an area roughly the size of the original thirteen colonies) is currently in a state of severe desertification, and twice that amount is threatened by it. "Desertification" is the drying out — and subsequent desolation — of land; it is caused by overdraft of groundwater, poor drainage of irrigated land, overgrazing, cultivation of erodible soil, and (nowadays) off-road vehicle damage. All of these forces are hard at work in the San Joaquin Valley, which is, quite literally, America's biggest food factory — it outproduces all but a few states, providing almost half of the nation's produce. Given its scanty rainfall, the Valley is 97 percent irrigated and pumps 1.5 million more acre-feet of water from its aquifers every year than can be replenished naturally (in order to satisfy one eighth of its total water consumption).

In San Luis Obispo County — almost none of which lies in the San Joaquin Valley — much land is now being purchased by people who have made money elsewhere and chosen to invest in agriculture as a tax shelter. The Hearst Corporation is the county's largest landholder, filling six pages on the assessor's rolls; other tracts are registered to such owners as Clint Eastwood, Joel McCrea, and William P. Clark. People primarily interested in protecting their investments find that the greatest financial returns are offered by intensive crops; San Luis Obispo County, for example, is now being planted heavily to wine grapes. With more and more such cultivation, farmers become more competitive for water, and wells are drilled deeper and deeper at increasingly high costs. As a result, growers of more traditional base crops like alfalfa (an acre of which requires four times as much water as do grapes) go out of business as the water supply evaporates. In Antelope Valley, one hour from Los Angeles, the groundwater table is dropping at a rate of 3 feet per year — largely because of the increasing *urban* demand for water. Such factors are what inspire Ian to describe modern agriculture as "cannibalism."

"Our agricultural resource is being mined out just as fast

as it can be," he said as we got back into the truck. "It's been squandered, just like petroleum."

We drove back up toward the house. When we were almost out of the bushy area above the dam, Ian said, "Oh boy, look at this one!" Up ahead, a rattlesnake was crossing the road. Ian gunned the engine and ran over the snake. Then he stopped and backed up to run over it again. From my window I saw the rattler crawling into the bushes, trailing a rope of red entrails.

When we got to the house, a woman with short black hair and Indian features stuck her head out the door. She asked Ian if he was ready, and he nodded. "I've got to cook some meat," he announced. We went around the side of the house to a barbecue pit. With the heel of his boot, Ian broke some bone-dry branches and put them in the pit. The dark-haired woman — Ian's wife, May — reappeared, wearing a grin and carrying a couple of home-grown steaks covered with herbs. "Yesterday we had a cottontail rabbit I trapped," said Ian. "I barbecue something about every day."

Ian set about grilling the steaks, pausing occasionally to profess. As he talked, he framed his points with his hands, his crooked finger creating a slightly skewed rhetorical impression. Standing by the smoking campfire, with the bare yellow hills and blue sky behind him, in his cowboy hat, rodeo belt, pink shirt, and pot belly, Ian represented a radical departure from the popular image of the down-jacketed, running-shoe-shod, urbane environmentalist.

We went inside. There were four wide-brimmed hats hanging from antlers, a half-dozen rifles in the corner, and several copies of *The Progressive* in a stand by the couch. I noticed that the switch plate had a picture of a quail on it. There was also a beautiful black-and-white photograph of a quail on the wall — a head and shoulders profile that Ian said he had taken with one hand while holding the bird in the other. (Ian's stationery is also decorated with pictures of quail.) The view from the dining room table was to the west, down Ian's canyon, a series of brown-green furrowed hills culminating in the blue Santa Lucias. The sky was slightly faint at the horizon. May had set the table with copious quantities of food — beans, corn, carrots, potato salad, salsa for the steaks, a plate of frozen cookies. After we'd made a dent in the meal, I asked Ian about Starker Leopold.

"Starker was a loving, delightful, patient, considerate, optimistic fella," Ian said. "But we found a contrast between his philosophy and his old man's. Starker said quail had to be fit in, that they were second to economic use of the land. My position is the other way around: economic use has to be fit in to the ecosystem. I don't believe in burning oak trees to make room for cattle *or* for quail. In *A Sand County Almanac*, Aldo Leopold used the oak as a sacred plant in the saga of the atom going into the ground and traveling from organism to organism. But Starker was recommending eradication of the blue oak. Tree shade reduces the fertility of the ground; if you let the sun in, grass will grow. But shrubs and chaparral break up the rock and work with it to form topsoil — they build a fertilizer that will eventually support grassland again. Fire is just a short-term solution. It puts energy into a nonavailable form. Not many top experts look at the smoke of a range fire as energy."

"Didn't the Indians burn their land?"

"The proposition seems to be that we ought to go back to the aboriginal state. The Indians didn't necessarily know any better than we do."

Now I asked about the fight Ian had had with another Defenders of Wildlife board member. He chuckled.

"They'd changed their name from Defenders of Furbearers to Defenders of Wildlife, but they weren't doing much about wildlife," he said. "They were mostly worrying about horses, dogs, and cattle. In a lot of ways they were working along the same lines I was, but they were protectionists and I was a hunter. Genetically, we are hunters — it's in our origins. Anyhow, I was in the office talking to the board president about 1080; after its ban as a predicide, people thought we'd seen the last of it, but its use as a rodenticide was far more lethal — they were dumping it from planes. This other board member came in and overheard us. He said, 'You're wrong about that, Ian.' He was a successful wildlife photographer, and he was making a film on endangered species. The Fish and Wildlife Service had taken him into the oil country around Taft — where there's no livestock to begin with, so no need for predator control — and convinced him that 1080 wasn't being used in the habitat of the kit fox. But I knew it was; and for that matter, I didn't think a Defenders board member should be having business dealings with the Fish and Wildlife Service; we were really uptight then about situations that might seem to represent a conflict of interest.

"He called me a liar. He said, 'You're gonna destroy this whole organization.' He went kinda *ber*-serk, and he charged me. I got — whaddya call it — a headlock on him. We went over a table and a couple of chairs." Thinking about it, Ian started shaking with laughter. "By golly, we tore that office around."

After lunch, Ian said he had to go out and "check on a few things." I stayed behind at the house to look through some of his scrapbooks. Eventually I came upon this clipping from the March 30, 1967, *San Francisco Chronicle*:

DIABLO POWER PLANT OPPOSED

SAN LUIS OBISPO–Pacific Gas and Electric Company's proposed coastal power plant at Diablo Canyon was attacked yesterday as a threat to the "total environment" of northern California.

Ian I. McMillan, Shandon rancher and prominent conservation leader, urged the State Public Utilities Commission to defer approval of the plan pending an expert, independent study of its potential effect on "the human ecology."

He said the plant would bring tremendous population growth and with it industrial development and "smog, the disease of an industrial civilization."

McMillan testified as PUC representatives resumed hearings here on the nuclear plant proposal. His was the first prolonged attack on the plant, which has drawn massive endorsement from civic and governmental groups for its salutary effect on tax base and employment.

Other clippings from the *San Luis Obispo Telegram Tribune* and *Paso Robles Daily Press* followed:

"Ian McMillan Files Resume with AEC to Protest PG&E Plant."

"Ian McMillan Accepted as Adversary."

"Ian McMillan Drops Bombshell into PUC Hearings on PG&E Plant."

"Who Is Ian McMillan? AEC Shows Need to Know More about California."

"Proposed City of 25,000 on Coast Is Plan Says I. McMillan."

To anyone remotely familiar with the Diablo Canyon nuclear power plant controversy, which has resulted in the arrest of thousands of protesters over the past decade, these clippings read like the lyrics to an anthem, like the chronicle of an awakening . . . maybe the screenplay of a movie. The story of Ian's involvement with Diablo is not that different from the plot of *High Noon*, wherein a brave and solitary cowboy stands on his principles against the townspeople, ultimately winning them over to his side but losing his respect for them in the process. (The difference is that, in the movie, Gary Cooper won.)

*

In 1962, Pacific Gas and Electric, then the nation's second largest investor-owned utility, began negotiating to buy land for a nuclear power plant on the central California coast. The first site the company targeted was the Nipomo Dunes, near Pismo Beach, but PG&E abandoned that idea when the Sierra Club voted to oppose the construction of power plants in places with high recreational or scenic value. The company had previously lost a fight to build a nuclear plant at Bodega Bay, north of San Francisco, and now PG&E was willing to negotiate — so willing, in fact, that Sierra Club president Will Siri was invited to join in the selection of a new site.

On retiring from the club presidency in 1966, Siri — a nuclear physicist at the Lawrence Berkeley Laboratory — recommended Diablo Canyon as a satisfactory alternative to the Nipomo Dunes. This still ran counter to the Sierra Club's stated policy, as Diablo Canyon was part of the last untrammeled stretch of California coastline between Mexico and Mendocino — it contained a forest of ferns and coast live oaks, a year-round stream, and a natural cove full of tidepools, kelp beds, sea lions, and abalone. David Brower, then the Sierra Club's executive director, recommended that the board postpone its decision until after its members had had a chance to visit the site (the only director who had done so was out of the country), but the board — apparently as eager to bargain with PG&E as the utility was to curry favor with environmentalists — rejected his suggestion. Siri's motion was seconded by the photographer Ansel Adams, and the Sierra Club's board of directors endorsed the idea of a nuclear power plant at Diablo Canyon.

At the time, Ian McMillan was chairman of the advisory board for Montana de Oro State Park, which occupies a section of coastline just north of Diablo Canyon. Unbowed by the official logic — whether PG&E's or the Sierra Club's — Ian began scrutinizing plans for the plant "on the grounds

that they weren't fully and properly explaining what it was
going to do, and whether or not we needed it. Its specified
design and purpose was for an urban environment growing
and doubling in size every ten years. But it was in an agricultural area! We were told that agriculture would have its
burden lifted and that the schools would profit; people
thought Diablo would lower their taxes. But it seemed to me
that if we had the kind of growth that the plant was designed
to propagate, we'd just be that much worse off than we already were. The three facilities of growth are transportation,
water, and power. My question was whether this growth was
in the public interest."

In the first hearings before the state Public Utilities Commission, PG&E was required to show that the plant was necessary, safe, and economical. At the meeting described in the
Chronicle clipping, Ian delivered a lengthy statement in which
he maintained "that the present supply of electric power in
central California is already facilitating, and is generally
serving to sustain and propagate, a wild, unregulated growth
of a general human establishment that in its random prolif-
eration is destroying, at an accelerating rate, its basic environmental resources." He produced a newspaper clipping
showing that the local Chamber of Commerce had recently
mailed out a thousand letters advertising the San Luis
Obispo area's smog-free climate (the only example of such
remaining in south-central California) to industries in Los
Angeles, encouraging them to relocate. He pointed out that
smog — "the new by-product of economic growth and the
new criterion of human density," which had already been
shown to damage crops in the Central Valley — would necessarily increase as a result of growth fueled by the "clean"
energy provided by a nuclear power plant.

None of Ian's early objections to Diablo stemmed from the
dangers of nuclear power. "The 'peaceful atom' was a plau-
sible argument when it first came out," he remembers. Even

Brower of the Sierra Club was pro-nuke at the time. But as Ian's interest in the issue intensified, he began "doing homework." He read *The Careless Atom* by Sheldon Novick and *Perils of the Peaceful Atom* by Richard Curtis and Elizabeth Hogan. He attended Atomic Energy Commission hearings, where he saw "the top men in nuclear physics sitting around arguing about how many grams of radiation you could release, whether infants would be more susceptible to it, how many miles around the plant you wouldn't want to drink the milk. You could see as clearly as anything that they didn't know what they were getting into — they were guessing. It was a monstrosity." Ian procured a study by John Gofman and Arthur Tamplin that had been commissioned by the AEC; it said that near the Hanford, Washington, nuclear plant, which discharged its cooling water into the Columbia River, the radioactivity of river plankton was 2,000 times greater than that of the water. Duck egg yolks were 40,000 times more radioactive, swallows, 75,000 times, caddis fly larvae, 350,000 times more radioactive than the river water near the plant.

Ian remembered an incident during World War II when a Japanese submarine surfaced off Santa Barbara and shelled oil installations onshore; he wondered what the consequences would have been if the target had been a nuclear power plant standing on the bluffs just above the beach. He was also concerned about earthquakes. A friend introduced him to Ralph Vrana, a geology instructor at California Polytechnic College in San Luis Obispo, who had studied the area offshore from Diablo Canyon. Vrana told Ian that the region harbored a number of faults that hadn't shown up in the official reports and that it had been the center of some forty earthquakes during a six-month period in 1969. (PG&E's geological consultants had, in fact, previously overlooked earthquake faults in studies for plants at Bodega Bay, Point Arena, and San Onofre, and its nuclear facilities at

Vallecitos and Humboldt Bay had actually been shut down because of tardily discovered faults.) At Ian's request, Vrana testified at the AEC seismic hearings, and the U.S. Geological Survey was consequently commissioned to restudy the area offshore from Diablo Canyon. The USGS had found evidence of faulting there in 1968 but had not made the discovery public; after its 1970 restudy, it did announce the existence of northwest-trending faults in the area. However, since Vrana had suggested the presence of *northeast*-trending faults, the investigations were discontinued, and the seismic issue could no longer be raised until PG&E applied for an operating license.

In 1973, a student on a USGS field trip heard about an offshore fault that had been mapped in 1969 by two Shell Oil geologists, Ernest Hoskins and John R. Griffiths, who had published their findings in 1971. Several USGS geologists later admitted that they had known about the "Hosgri" Fault and had discussed it with the AEC. According to the minutes of a 1967 meeting of PG&E, the AEC, the USGS, and Westinghouse, PG&E's geological consultant, Professor Richard Jahns of Stanford University, had warned the company of the possible existence of a large, active earthquake fault 2 miles offshore from Diablo Canyon; but Jahns and PG&E still asserted that they did not intend to relocate the plant or "do further trenching at the risk of uncovering geologic structures which could lead to additional speculation and possibly delay the project." In 1970, when Vrana asked Jahns at an AEC hearing whether he thought all geologic and seismic risks near the plant had been uncovered, Jahns replied that they had. PG&E and the AEC maintained that the nearest oceanic fault of any significance was 50 miles away. No public mention was made of the Hosgri Fault, and work on the power plant continued.

In 1975, the USGS finally reported that the Hosgri Fault might be connected to the San Simeon, San Gregorio, and

Big Sur faults, could be 400 miles long, and was capable of causing a 7.5-magnitude earthquake. The Diablo plant was designed to withstand a quake of only 6.75, ten times weaker than one that the Hosgri could generate.* When the Nuclear Regulatory Commission was informed of this fact, Richard DeYoung, its assistant director of light water reactor licensing, hoped that the USGS would revise its findings: "The impact of potential denial for operation of a plant approved for construction cannot be underestimated," he wrote. Later, DeYoung told the *Los Angeles Times* that a permit for the plant might never have been issued if the Hosgri Fault had come to light when the plant was still waiting for a construction permit, but "when we look at the operating license stage, where a billion dollars' worth of plant was just sitting there, designed on bases with which we concurred, you can't take the same approach as you could when $32 million was spent."

In 1984 a team of geologists from San Diego, after studying the area offshore from Diablo Canyon, put forth the theory that the Hosgri is not a vertical strike-slip fault similar to the San Andreas but rather a diagonal "thrust" fault that surfaces offshore. If this theory proves correct, it is probable that the Hosgri Fault passes directly beneath Diablo Canyon.

After the discovery of the Hosgri Fault, local attitudes toward Diablo Canyon underwent a marked change. The *San*

---

* The plant's earthquake safety criteria were upgraded after the discovery of the Hosgri Fault, and the facility is now designed to survive a 7.5 earthquake. Throughout the years of hearings on the safety of Diablo Canyon, however, earthquakes occurred in various parts of California, indicating that greater ground motion than previously thought possible could result from relatively small quakes. In 1971, a 6.5 earthquake struck the San Fernando Valley, killing sixty-five people; its peak ground acceleration of 1.25 g was previously unheard of. The Diablo plant, originally designed to withstand a ground movement of 0.4 g, is now built for a peak ground acceleration of 0.75 g 3 miles away. Ground motion for a 7.5 quake, however, has never been recorded at a distance less than 25 miles.

Luis Obispo Telegram Tribune went on record as opposing the plant, and in 1977 forty-seven protesters were arrested for occupying it. Among them was Ian McMillan — age seventy-one.

"I had been telling young people that, if they wanted a future, they had to get involved in physical confrontations," Ian said when he came back from his chores. "Pretty soon they called me up and asked me if I wanted to join them. By golly no, I didn't want to join them, but I couldn't very well say no — it'd be like a lieutenant telling his troops, 'Boys, you get on out there and fight, but I'm gonna stay here.' I went down to San Luis Obispo three times to drill and prepare. I've never been part of anything where there was as much talent as there was in that. We acted out a play about a possible breakdown; they were teaching us to be nonviolent, even if somebody spit in your face or slapped you. That didn't exactly square with the way I'd learned things.

"On the day we got arrested, the regular gate was blocked, so we had to get a stepladder and climb over a chain-link fence. We walked darn near a mile with our camping gear and supplies." Ian — a horseman, not a hiker — started laughing. "I was pretty glad to see those cops coming."

During the pretrial hearings it was discovered that two of the "protesters" in Ian's group had been police agents, and the California Supreme Court dropped the charges on the grounds of violation of lawyer-client confidentiality. Ian, however, had pleaded no contest to trespassing; he was fined $500 and spent five days in jail.

"We had seventeen people in an eight-man cell. A lot of guys didn't like the mush they gave us for breakfast, so they threw it out through the bars. One guy went off his rocker and started howling at night. Another guy hung himself a couple of cells away — that was a big commotion. I wouldn't particularly want to go through it again. To a lot of people, it was just terrible for a person in my position to go get arrested with a bunch of hippies; I still get anonymous letters saying, 'Boy, we're ashamed of you, Ian.' That don't bother me one particle." In 1973, when Ian had less company in his opposition to Diablo Canyon, he had quoted Robert Service in a letter to the *Telegram Tribune:* "In fear of their lives/Or because of their wives/They were shunned by the best of their pals."

The following year, 478 people were arrested for occupying or blockading the plant. Two months after their mass sentencing, the nuclear plant at Three Mile Island in Pennsylvania came close to a meltdown (and, for the first time, the Sierra Club went on record opposing Diablo Canyon). In June of 1979, 40,000 people attended a Stop Diablo rally in San Luis Obispo. In September of 1981, when the facility was scheduled to begin loading fuel, 1,901 protesters — their ranks now including politicians, film stars, and rock musicians — were arrested during a two-week blockade of the site. On the last day of the protest, a junior pipe analyst discovered that the wrong blueprint had been used to build safety equipment for the reactor — the major earthquake supports were installed backward. The NRC suspended Diablo's license while Bechtel Corporation engineers found and fixed more than 3,000 errors in the plant.

By 1984 — due to enormous cost overruns, including the price of Bechtel's repairs and the upgrading of earthquake safety design criteria — more than a third of PG&E's assets were tied up in Diablo Canyon. The plant, originally estimated to cost $152 million, has to date cost the company $5.8 billion. In 1986, PG&E requested a rate increase of $1.3 billion to pay for its first full year of owning and operating the plant.

It was getting late in the afternoon, and Ian offered to drive me back to Eben's place. As we turned from his driveway onto the Gillis Canyon Road, he told me that he is no longer a member of any environmental organization except the Cooper Ornithological Society, in which he holds an honorary lifetime membership. He has given up on Audubon, the Sierra Club, Defenders of Wildlife, et al. "They're just too far from the center of things," he said. I asked him whether he thought that, owing to his unwillingness to compromise, he might have isolated himself from the environmental movement.

"I haven't isolated myself!" he said. "The movement has moved off and left me. Let's face it — the causes and forces I've worked and fought for have been overwhelmed. As far as I can tell, if we'd all been out fishing it wouldn't have made any difference. Look at the people in public office now. You've heard of James Watt? Ronald Reagan? It's nothing short of shocking. Up to about fifteen years ago, I would have said the machinery of government was working; as we saw with 1080, if you had the facts you'd win. But that was under Nixon. Now Reagan has brought 1080 back. How could anybody say a society that would elect Reagan over Carter is anything other than a total loss? The system has broken down. The world has changed; I haven't. I'm an environmentalist, and it's my view that the world has gone crazy."

We stopped at the grove where I'd seen the coyote. Ian said it was the site of the old Gillis homestead; at the turn of the century, Napoleon ("Polie") Gillis had built the adobe hut, tunneled into the hill for water, and planted the trees. "Sometimes there are forty or fifty nests here," Ian said as we walked into the grove. "There's a pair of redtailed hawks, a pair of horned owls, a pair of shrikes, one of Say's phoebes, two orioles, five house finches, five Lawrence goldfinches, probably fifteen mourning doves. Right now I can hear three different kingbirds." He reached up and grabbed a branch. "This is a blackbird nest. There's probably nothing in it." He pulled the branch down gently; inside the twisted nest were five tiny balls of down with open mouths on top.

"Ecology is an odd thing," Ian said as we got back into the truck. "It's a field of reason that's easy for some people to dig, and near impossible for others. They can understand profound philosophical systems, but not simple laws of survival. Ninety percent of the system on my place just comes from a feeling for how survival works. When you're working to develop quail, you're practicing the same social things that benefit the condor. I can't think of *anything* that illustrates the principles of survival better than the condor. You read Darwin, you read Malthus, Justus Liebig, David Lack — *The Natural Regulation of Animal Numbers*. We need to teach ecology the way we teach mathematics — to bring people to an understanding of the condor's role and to develop a feeling for it. A land ethic, as Aldo Leopold said."

We pulled up in front of Eben's house and sat talking for a few more minutes. Unseen by Ian, Eben emerged from the barn; he came up behind the truck and slapped the tailgate as if to test its reliability. For a few minutes he stood outside Ian's window while the two brothers — the bull and the badger — discussed their neighbors' crops. Ian gazed off through his windshield; Eben looked beyond the tailgate. They didn't look at each other.

Ian said he had to get back. "I'm writing a letter to Senator Cranston about Reagan's acreage reduction program. It's taking me a couple of days. Last week I sent one to the task force on predator control." So: despite the defeats, and his consequent pessimism and negativity, Ian was still at it — hammering out letter after letter, still stubbornly trying to save the world despite its unceasing deterioration. In many ways — his political activism, his adoption of quail, his love of the West as expressed in his writing and in his cowboy style — Ian struck me as more romantic than Eben. As the saying goes, the biggest cynic is a frustrated romantic.

Before getting out, I asked Ian how he managed to stave off discouragement while fighting losing battles.

"You're discouraged to begin with," he said. "But the fact that you're here at all means you're committed to fighting, despite its being discouraging. Unless you fight, there'd be no chance of saving anything."

That night during dinner, a battered white pickup driven by a Mexican farmworker came up the road and stopped beside the spreading atriplex bush at the bottom of Eben's driveway. "He's looking to see if there are any rattlesnakes under that bush," Eben observed from the table. "Mexicans have a morbid fear of snakes. Out on the Carrisa Plains, I used to tell those Mexican cowboys stories at night. I'd say I'd found a dead sheep and seen something coiled beside it — I'd build it up to a real critical point, you know. Finally I'd say it was a great ... big ... RATTLESNAKE! Boy, they'd jump when I said rattlesnake."

Gladys was looking out the window at the truck. "He sees one," she said. "He's backing up. Oh, look, he ran over it!" From a distance we could see the coiled serpent shining in the sun; it slithered away under the atriplex bush. The truck departed, and Gladys went down the driveway with a stick to look for the snake.

"Isn't that funny," Eben remarked. "That guy will tear down the road in his truck and never even think about the danger, but more people are killed by automobiles in one day than have been killed by rattlesnakes in the history of the state. Usually in summer we'll have about six rattlesnakes come in around the house. I think one might bite you if you stepped on it, but I wouldn't bet on it — they only bite what they can eat, and you aren't edible. But Gladys doesn't like them, especially if the grandchildren are around. I don't like to kill animals if you're not accomplishing anything; if you kill a rattlesnake, another one will take its place — the population stays the same. So I'll get them running, pick them up with a shovel, and let them fall off. Then I pick them up and drop them again. They're a heavy snake — they make a big bang when they hit the ground. Well, a rattlesnake isn't a damn fool; by about the third time, they stay on the shovel. I take them up to the water trough. I kept six or seven for a year or two, just for interest. They don't take much food. They were breeding in there. One female had eight young.

"If you asked the average person, 'How close do you think you're related to a rattlesnake?' their reaction would be revulsion. But they aren't really that different; they were far more sophisticated than I expected from a reptile. You wouldn't normally believe that snakes would 'make love,' but they showed a tendency toward affection and tenderness in copulation that they didn't show any other time, except for maybe when the mother was taking care of the young. Even if you learn these things from reading, there's a different dimension to observing it yourself. It becomes more important. If you observe it, you become a part of it — you see our relationship to animals when you see them in conditions like that."

IN 1967, Eben and Gladys went to Australia. Eben gave a
lecture in Hawaii for the Audubon Society, then they flew to
American Samoa and took a tramp steamer loaded with
copra through the Tongan Islands. Along the way, the boat
kept stopping to pick up islanders who were going to a coronation — the queen of Tonga had just died and was to be
succeeded by her son. Eben was sitting in the doorway of his
stateroom one day when he was approached by a portly
Tongan wearing a grass skirt. The man said his name was
Tweeta, and he asked Eben if he would mind answering
some questions about America for the other Tongans.

"The main thing they wanted to know about was freeways," Eben says. "They'd heard about these giant roads
going in six or seven different directions. I drew a map showing an on ramp and an off ramp and tried to give them an

honest explanation of the dangers and everything. I told them that the cars went a mile in one minute — the old boat captain had a stopwatch and ticked it off. That really bamboozled 'em. I told them about tall trees like the redwoods, and they could kind of fathom that; I said they were about four boat lengths high. But the next morning they asked me about freeways all over again. They just couldn't get it through their heads how so many automobiles going that fast — four rows in one direction and four in another — wouldn't smash into each other."

Tweeta apparently could read barometric pressure with the soles of his feet. "I'd come along and ask him what the reading was that day," says Eben. "He'd tell me, and I'd shout up to the captain, and invariably old Tweeta would be right." Just before they arrived at the main island, he invited Eben and Gladys to the coronation, offering to build them a house. As they were already behind in their itinerary, the McMillans declined the offer and continued on to Fiji. Tweeta had mentioned that he needed a Hohner harmonica in the key of E, so Eben bought one in the Fiji free market and sent it back with the boat captain. At the market, a young Indian tried to sell Gladys a pair of cat's-eye earrings; Eben accused him of trying to pawn off something that he'd gotten cheap in Hong Kong.

"He took umbrage," says Eben. "He kind of cried, then he got mad. He said that they made the earrings right there on the island, and insisted that we go up and look at the factory with him. He gave us some jewelry, and the next day he and his uncle showed us around the town. We took them out to dinner. I'd always heard that they showed their appreciation of a meal by belching; I thought it was probably a falsehood, but I was kind of looking at them out of the corner of my eye — I wasn't going to let anything pass me by. Sure enough, when they got done they pushed their chairs back, and out came three or four of the biggest belches you ever heard."

When they got back to their rooming house, Eben and Gladys were surprised to find the princess of Tonga and her entourage — they had come to Fiji to buy clothes for the coronation. "Pretty soon one of the ladies came to our room and asked if we'd like to sing with them," says Eben. "We came out into this living room area — there were no chairs, and nobody spoke English. We sat cross-legged on the floor and sang up a storm. We just tried to stay with them and follow the tones. Boy, were they smiling! Except for the princess — she just sat there like a wax woman. She had a professional jester trying to entertain her, but she never cracked a smile."

To get to Australia, Eben and Gladys took a lumber schooner (which sank on its return voyage). In Sydney they rented a Volkswagen bus in which they planned to tour the continent, making a wildlife film for Audubon. Eben had a letter from Starker Leopold introducing him to Harry Frith, the head of the wildlife research division of the Commonwealth Scientific and Industrial Research Organization; Frith at the time was making a study of Australian pigeons, and he had succeeded in trapping every species but one — the flock pigeon. "He said that you could always recognize them because they look like they're shining a light at you," says Eben. "They have this white spot on their forehead. So we're driving along and a flock of pigeons goes by, heading for this dried-up lake. I snuck down there with my camera and stuck my head up, and the first thing I saw was a bunch of white spots a-looking at me. When we got to the Constable station, I called Harry Frith, and the next day he sent a plane up there and trapped five birds." When Eben and Gladys got back to Canberra, Harry Frith was a-burst with praise.

On their first night outside Sydney, the McMillans drove

down a dirt road off the highway looking for a place to sleep. "We saw this dusty old car at a camp spot," says Eben. "Gladys said, 'Don't stop here — they'll slit our throats.' I said, 'Well, we can slit throats too.' So we stopped and ate dinner. Pretty soon I saw some people. The guy's hands were covered with pot grease, and he had a dirty-looking beard. They were pretty jolly; I figured they'd probably had about three or four belts of whiskey. I sauntered over, and it turned out they'd just made a full circle of Australia in exactly the opposite direction from the one we were going in. They had all the information we needed. I told the guy I wanted to photograph aboriginal populations, and he said, 'I'm just the fella who can help you.' He wrote me out a letter and said, 'Go to the office of aboriginal affairs and tell this guy I sent you.' Back at our campsite I said to Gladys, 'I've met a lot of fakers in my life, but there's the champion.' He really sounded like a bull-thrower — the kind of guy who'd tell you anything just to make you feel good.

"I took the whole thing pretty lightly, but when we got up to Darwin I went to this office — which is kind of like the offices of public transportation in Sacramento — and it turned out that the guy whose name was on the letter was the director. His secretary said he was busy. I said, 'Okay. But I've got this letter of introduction, so at least he'll know we're here.' She took the letter in, and by golly he came right out and invited us into his office. Turned out this fella in the Outback was the PR man for the senator from that part of the country — he was kind of a kingmaker, and he'd gotten this director his job. The boss-man sent us down to the aboriginal reserve the next day. He put down on the forms that we were 'behaviorists' from America."

In three months, the McMillans drove their rented bus 15,000 miles — "through the dust and everything else" — on a counterclockwise circuit of Australia. They camped at waterholes, collected plants, and saw kangaroos every day, which was sometimes three or four times as often as they saw other cars. At Eighty-Mile Beach, near Pardue Sands on the west coast, the bus stalled and the transmission jammed. Eben says, "It was about the worst predicament we were ever in — stuck out there a hundred miles from any habitation. Then I heard the purr of an engine. At first I thought it was an airplane, but it was a Chevy. This guy and this woman were coming along — he was an engineer who lived three hundred miles away. He said a truck would probably come by within a couple of days. But then he tried pulling on the gearshift. By golly, he pulled on it until his face turned red. All of a sudden the gearshift popped back out. From then on we just rolled — five hundred miles across the Nullarbor Plain. The whole trip was one of those situations where you just seem to have all the luck."

Eben had wanted to go to Australia because of its geographical similarity to North America. "I thought I'd be able to understand it," he says. "And as soon as we got into the interior, where there were windmills, I felt right at home — I knew what was going to happen before it happened. But in the tropics my head was going around all the time. I was like a kid at a circus — everything was new, and I couldn't zero in on anything. I couldn't interpret: 'What role does this thing play?' We saw barn owls hunting in the middle of the day! Protective coloration hasn't played as much of a part in evolution there; here, a horned lark could be thirty feet away and you'd never see it, but there, a bunch of pink parrots would rise up all of a sudden — it upsets you. You say, 'My God, what's going on? They don't have to hide?' Here everything is aggressive, but a predator in the tropics is not an interloper. He's accepted. When a hawk dives into a flock of parrots, they don't scatter; they know it'll only eat *one*, and they calm down again within twenty seconds. In the tropics they don't need that acute sense of self-preservation, because there are other factors working toward a balance.

"Tropical species are very specialized. They're not competitive, because they've had such a long time to work out their relationships — everything has its niche. The farther you get away from the tropics, the more disorderly things become because of ice. In the Arctic, lots of species are just fresh back since the ice receded, and they haven't had time to reach equilibrium. You see tremendous fluctuations in species there — the snowshoe hare, the Arctic fox, snowy owls, lemmings. . . . There are times when you can set out traps and not catch a single lemming, and other times the whole landscape is moving with them. It's tremendously cyclic — the populations just crash. As a general rule, when predators crash, it's because of malnutrition; when there are too many of them, they start eating each other. A good indication of healthy land is an abundant number of species, not an abundance of one specie. Someday we're going to find out that the vast herds in Africa are a declining condition; it just goes against nature. I argue that the great herds of buffalo in North America were something new under the sun — they came from the Indian burning the prairie. I bet the Indian never started setting fires until he got the horse. If he had, a fire might just as apt get him as the buffalo."

Eben calls the continental United States, situated as it is about halfway between the Equator and the Arctic, "about half-orderly." From the vantage point of his window, he is making an ongoing study of its ecological equilibrium. Recently, during a rainy year, a gray fox stumbled upon the meal ticket that Eben's ranch represents and set up housekeeping immediately; a fox, after all, is no fool. "Pretty soon," remembers Eben, "the quail were gone, the roadrunners were gone, the thrashers were gone, the rabbits were gone. I had to trap him and take him somewhere else. He was just the picture of intelligence, a bundle of speed — that big tail they have seems to act as a rudder. But he was too successful. A tropical predator specie would *never* get to the point where it would endanger the species it depends on.

"Now there are too many rabbits here. Their average life-span is probably about two months. When the population gets too high, they start building up parasites — ticks in their ears and things like that. You can see the young ones gradually weaken. They start fighting among themselves — one rabbit will charge another and jump over it, and the bottom one squirts a little stream of urine that gets on the stomach of the jumper. It irritates them tremendously — it discourages them from gathering in groups and eliminates density. Predation is necessary to weed out the weak and the sick. When you have a system like what I've got, natural predation doesn't work very well because it's inhibited by our presence. In order to maintain the natural ecology, I have to take the place of predators. Chances are, when I shoot rabbits, I don't do a real good job of simulating a predator; it's *pretty* much the same, but not quite as efficient as a bobcat springing — then they all scatter, and the weak one makes the bobcat a meal."

The bobcat, another temporary lodger, hunted rabbits on the lawn while Eben and Gladys watched through the window. They saw the cat catch thirteen rabbits over a period of six months, and Eben thinks it probably got four times that many when they weren't looking. "He maintained the rabbit population at its minimum carrying capacity. It was a tremendous spectacle — just like a finely tuned watch. The two have evolved together to where a good healthy rabbit will outcompete a bobcat; the rabbit knows it and the bobcat knows it. A bobcat has to be very keen to catch a rabbit. When he was getting ready to charge, his whole body took on the appearance of readiness and nervousness — his ears tipped down, his eyes would gleam. He seemed full of hate. The rabbit, sitting there watching this, knows when he's got to run. And the bobcat won't make his run until he's pretty sure he's gonna be successful. I've never seen a bobcat go after a rabbit that was watching it; if he charges and misses, he'll alert five other rabbits — they see what they need to do to beat him. Plus, he burns up energy that he isn't getting back. If the balance is at a fine point, the bobcat isn't going to find his job easy.

"Anybody who doesn't think there's a plan for these things doesn't begin to understand them," Eben continues. "We think we need to analyze things, but there are forces we just can't explain. What enabled that bobcat to catch just enough rabbits to stay alive without destroying the population? Not natural selection; if survival of the fittest went on, pretty soon a bobcat would be able to jump fifty feet and a rabbit could run two hundred miles an hour. *Environmental balance* is more important than natural selection. Every force has an opposite force — there's a seesaw effect, a Law of the Median, that's been at work since there's been a universe. Everything that grows and produces energy has to do it for a purpose. It would be a waste for a plant to grow and not have anything to eat it, to carry on that energy cycle from carbon back to carbon again. It's all for the benefit of the soil; it might go through a hundred phases before it gets back into the ground, but in the end it produces the green plant, which is the basis of all life.

"With man, very little of that energy is getting back into the soil. Hundreds of thousands of tons of garbage goes out to sea every week. We're writing checks without depositing anything into our account. And we're going badly into debt."

*

Eben has borrowed money twice in his life: once to buy cattle and once to buy a car. He paid both loans back within ninety days. He has two credit cards: one from the telephone company and one from Sears. He turned in his American Express card because he didn't like being charged $12 a year for it. When his bank began assessing a fee for his checking account, Eben took the bill into Paso Robles and told the manager of the bank, "You've got two choices — you can cross that off of there, or I can write you a check right now for the whole amount of the account." He hasn't paid for checking since.

To say that Eben and Gladys are frugal is like saying that Death Valley can get warm at times. When they finish using plastic bags, they wash them, hang them on the clothesline to dry, and use them again. Eben visits water holes and collects spent shotgun shells, then trims them with his knife and refills them with shot. When he and Gladys go to town, they take sandwiches with them: "All you're doing when you eat in a restaurant is paying somebody wages to cook for you," Gladys explains. Eben once told me he was going to remove the catalytic converter from his truck "and just throw it away. The thing has to heat up before it works, and I don't ever get my rig running long enough for it to heat up. If the state fines me, I'm gonna challenge 'em on it." The next time I saw him I asked what he'd done about the converter. He said he hadn't done anything. "We've had so much clear weather since they put on that requirement, I figure I ought to play along until I can prove I know any better."

Such reversals in light of additional evidence are not atypical of Eben. One time he went to an optometrist who charged him $60 for a checkup and prescribed a pair of glasses that cost another $60. "The glasses didn't work," says Eben. "Three weeks later I was seeing worse. So I went back to the guy and said, 'I needed the checkup, but I think you ought to give me a refund on the glasses.' He wouldn't do it. I told him I was used to getting raw deals, but not from somebody who's supposed to be a professional. There's so much reverence for doctors — when I left, the people in the waiting room looked like they thought I'd murdered him. Now I'm gonna take an ad out in the paper. If they'll print it, I'm going to say exactly what happened."

Later I asked Eben how the matter had been resolved. "Turned out the guy was right," he said. "A little while after that, I started seeing better." Nevertheless, he still maintains that for his "next vendetta, I'm going after the doctors. There are thousands of people languishing in penitentiaries who are a lot less crooked than physicians. You can tell you're gonna get soaked the minute you go in the office and see the way the guy looks at you. I had a little skin cancer removed a while ago; it took the doctor about thirty minutes, and he charged me eight hundred dollars. The old doctors I used to know would cut something like that off and charge you fifteen bucks."

In eighty years under the California sun, Eben has had some thirty skin cancers removed from his skull. He says that if he were ever to become debilitated by a disease, he wouldn't go to any expense to prolong his life: "If I got bedridden, I think that by mental suggestion I could keep pressing on it to where I'd bring about the end. When you get to the point where you can't produce as much as you consume, you have an obligation to step aside and make room for somebody else. People on a ranch don't think anything of going out and pulling the heads off chickens that aren't producing — it's what you've got to do to stay in business.

"I'd like to be a man who understood death the way he understood birth," says Eben. "My ambition while I live is to be able to die in a gentlemanly way — not whimpering or calling for the last straw, but recognizing just what death is.

I'd like to have enough presence of mind that I might get a pencil and relate some of it. But maybe you're not as much in control as you'd like to be. I remember this one tough old guy — when we'd play cards, he couldn't say one sentence without using profanity, but when he was dying he wanted a preacher in there to soften things up. Ernest Twisselmann got kind of afraid, I remember. I'd rather have a determined look than a blank stare. But maybe that's the stare of death."

TODAY IT'S cloudy. The temperature of the air has dropped. From the dining room table, Eben examines a scattering of grasshoppers in the mint bush outside his window.

"I'd like to know the life cycle of these grasshoppers if this cool weather continues," he says. "I noticed yesterday, when it was warm, every one of those stems had a grasshopper on it. I think this is a three- or four-year cyclic irruption. Most cyclic insects are not long-lived; they get kind of lethargic when it's cold. Cyclic irruptions are like diseases — people with rheumatism wear a copper ring or drink tea made from grape leaves and the rheumatism goes away, probably because it was near the end of its cycle anyway. In Salt Lake City they've got a California gull on the Utah state capitol because the seagulls destroyed a plague of crickets that were eating the Mormons' gardens. My guess would be that those crickets' cycle had just about run its course.

"A few years back it was the Mediterranean fruit fly. For hundreds of years we're going along, and all of a sudden here comes the Medfly to scare the dickens out of everybody. I didn't involve myself with it at all. There was so much probability of its being a farce — a ploy to embarrass the administration. It was all out of order. The main thing the Medfly showed was the extent of mind control today."

The Mediterranean fruit fly — *Ceratitus capitata*, a species that has spread from its original home in Africa to Europe, Asia, Australia, Central and South America, and Hawaii — threatened to establish itself in northern California in 1980 and 1981 before it disappeared coincidentally with the spraying of 192,000 gallons of malathion over ten million acres, the stripping and buying of 1,150 tons of fruit from 100,000 urban backyards, the seizure of 98,000 pieces of produce from five million automobiles, the quarantine of an area of 3,500 square miles, and the expenditure of over $100 million. It nevertheless earned a place in history as (a) the first environmental near-disaster to be brought on by excessive caution and (b) the itsy-bitsy insect that buried Governor Jerry Brown, who refused to allow aerial pesticide-spraying for a year after the Medfly's presence was detected. Since California grows almost half of the country's produce, the Medfly — which lays its eggs in more than 250 varieties of fruits and vegetables, causing them to rot — was said to represent not only a $1.4 billion threat to the state's agricultural industry but a potential booster of the Consumer Price Index as well. Therefore Brown's refusal to, in his words, "subject 500,000 people, including pregnant women, infants and children, to six or more aerial applications of a toxic pesticide" — followed by a reversal of this policy when the U.S. Department of Agriculture threatened a nationwide quarantine of California produce — was generally recognized as a nail in the governor's political coffin, already nine-tenths tight from his vacillation on such issues as Proposition 13 and the Peripheral Canal (a proposal to divert water south from northern California.)

Actually, Brown's terrestrial battle against the Medfly *had* included the spraying of chemical pesticides — by hand, from the ground — throughout the previous winter, together with the stripping of fruit and the release of sterile flies to abort reproduction in the wild population. These "integrated pest management" techniques succeeded in eradicating the Medfly from southern California and appeared to have worked in the north when no Medfly larvae were found there in the spring of 1981. Many scientists still believe that the outbreak of the following summer, which finally precipitated aerial spraying, resulted from the accidental release of nonsterile Peruvian flies along with the sterile ones. Numerous factors contributed to the failure of Brown's "boy scout tactics" (as the integrated approach was sarcastically labeled by *The New Republic*). For example, many homeowners refused to allow government employees onto their property, resulting in the ground treatment of as little as half of the infested area; and Baytex, the chemical initially used as a soil drench, was found to be less than fully effective but wasn't replaced by Diazinon for six months. While the Medflies discovered in southern California were identified within twenty-four hours and eradicated (through integrated techniques, including only one ground application of a chemical insecticide) shortly thereafter, the first flies trapped in the San Francisco Bay area — where cooler average winter temperatures were thought to prohibit the Medfly's permanent establishment — went unidentified for two weeks. By the time the northern infestation was accurately assessed, it covered hundreds of urban backyards and required the release of a billion sterile flies. Such large numbers of insects were, of necessity, analyzed hastily and procured from several sources — Hawaii, Mexico, Costa Rica, and Peru. Each place of origin had its own system for marking the flies, which made identification of them confusing in California (the blue-green dye used on pupae in Hawaii, for example, was very close to the color of the wild Medfly). Given the crisis conditions, in forty-eight hours of 1981 the government's anti-Medfly workforce increased from four hundred to four thousand employees, most of whom had no biological expertise and could not be trusted to accurately analyze either the flies or the traps, which were also accused of inefficiency, failing to attract the flies.

Nevertheless, "Governor Moonbeam" shouldered the blame — even though almost all of the directly affected communities had resisted aerial spraying. Gunshots were fired at helicopters when the bait applications began (the governor had an alibi), and $24 million worth of lawsuits were filed against the state for things like damaged paint on automobiles. Rather than the result of flaky politics, the Medfly brouhaha was the strongest illustration to date of the real conflict between urban and agricultural interests. The savvy insect was clever enough to establish itself in Silicon Valley, the home of a well-educated human population with a strong environmental (i.e., anti-pesticide) awareness. From the beginning, Brown's opposition on the Medfly question came not from the communities where the flies were found but rather from the state's enormous agricultural powers, which the Brown administration had already alienated by demanding environmental impact reports for pesticide programs. Jerry Brown was, in fact, a much bigger problem than the Medfly for the California pesticide industry, which exhibited considerable professional prowess in killing off both pests with one stone in the summer of 1981.

The question of whether aerial spraying really got rid of the Medfly remains more debatable than its effect on the vanished governor, however. The answer remains cloudy in

California, partly — and somewhat amazingly — because no significant studies of the Medfly population were performed during the crisis. Data from the enormous mark-release-recapture program, which might yield valuable information about the insect's population dynamics, have not been analyzed to this day. It is still unknown where the Medfly came from and whether it really disappeared because of aerial bait spraying or because the northern California winter of 1981–82 was colder and wetter than the one of 1980–81. The reason for this lack of information is that, when it comes to exotic pests, government control efforts are overwhelmingly oriented toward eradication — required by law under the California Food and Agricultural Code — rather than research. When the aim is total elimination of the population, there isn't any room for controlled, untreated plots to compare with areas that are sprayed.*

The question of malathion's real effect on the Medfly — or any pesticide's effect on any insect — is worth wondering about, as the main issue facing applied entomology today is the problem of pesticide resistance. Given that insects have been evolving defenses against natural pesticides in plants (for example, caffeine) for millions of years, natural selection can create immunity to manmade chemicals within a couple of generations, which occur over a few weeks. Widespread and highly adaptable species such as houseflies and

---

* In one of the few studies performed during the Medfly crisis, gardens in the spray area were found to harbor more mites, aphids, and whiteflies than comparable unsprayed plots, owing to the disappearance of these parasites' natural enemies. Gall midge populations in the town of Woodside reached populations ninety times greater than those in unsprayed areas, leading to the virtual destruction of some plants. Lower numbers and the decreased flight activity of bees reduced pollination and honey production. The types of aquatic insects in spray-monitored streams decreased by one third to one half, and malathion-contaminated storm runoff killed fish in a number of creeks.

cockroaches, for example, have survived the use of pesticides against them all over the world. A survey of California's twenty-five most serious agricultural pests — each of which caused more than $1 million worth of damage in 1970 — showed that seventeen were resistant to one or more classes of insecticides and twenty-four were either secondary outbreaks or resurgences worsened by the use of insecticides; in 1978 it was estimated that, despite a tenfold increase in the annual use of pesticides since 1942, the percentage of crops lost to insects in the United States had doubled, from 7 to 13 percent.

Given these facts, integrated pest management and biological control — that is, the human manipulation of what Eben would refer to as leavening factors (in this case, predators, pathogens, and parasitoids) — are acknowledged to hold the keys to pest control in the future. One indication of their growing role is that between 1972 and 1983 real sales of insecticides in the United States fell by an average of 4.7 percent per year. Since sales of *herbicides* have continued to rise steadily, it wouldn't be accurate to say that the pesticide industry's back is to the wall; nevertheless, observes Eben, "if I were hungry and out of work and knew where I could get a hold of some Mediterranean fruit flies, I don't think I'd be a bit backward about slipping 'em in and getting 'em going." The retail value of the malathion expended on the Medfly in California was nearly $3 million.

As it happens, the northern boundary for Medfly spraying in 1981 was the street where I live. For months the issue had been distant for me — as distant as San Jose is from Oakland, about 40 miles — but then sixteen Medflies, fourteen of them fertile, were found in my neighborhood in August. The helicopters came at night, once a week for six weeks. I stripped my lemon tree (it took two years for the fruit to come back), and my car still shows the tiny spots where the aerial bait spray hit. The poison was said to be one twenty-fifth the toxicity of my cat's flea collar. Nevertheless, it wasn't my choice to be sprayed from the sky with a chemical insecticide, and looking through the bedroom window at the helicopters flying in battle formation — so low that they shook the house, their red lights eerie against the night sky — I had a feeling that was repeated five years later after the Russian nuclear accident at Chernobyl. Namely: there is a tendency to be somewhat smug when one's protests are ignored and an accident happens far away. But as human evolution continues, the concept of "far away" has less and less application; with our assistance, fruit flies and/or nuclear fallout can travel the globe in a matter of hours. When they show up on your doorstep — as they must, sooner or later — smugness quickly becomes irrelevant. In the modern world, when one's fate is mandated by powers beyond one's control, distant problems can become immediate with astonishing rapidity.

Eben has to go to town. He needs to buy chicken wire. For the occasion, he has changed clothes. He now wears a long-sleeve white T-shirt, a red neckerchief, and maroon suede Etonic running shoes. In the morning sun, he whistles while doing chores before leaving — feeding the chickens, engaging the windmill, deploying a soaker hose in the garden. While performing the final operation, he notes that a quail has established a nest in a box around the base of a sage bush.

"Quail are a reproductive machine once they get going," Eben comments, bending over to turn on the hose. "The female lays fifteen eggs per mating. After the hatch, she turns the family over to the male and goes right out to find another mate. They go through this process four times and they can increase their population by three thousand percent. The

reason they have this ability is that they're a sedentary specie — very vulnerable to environmental stress. They have to
build up tremendous numbers to prepare for years when
some local factor might harm the population. When we had
a cold spell, the house finches went somewhere else, but the
mourning dove and quail populations just crashed.

"This is the lowest year for quail in recent memory on my
place. My son Greg thinks the roadrunners are eating them,
so he's started siccing his dog on the roadrunners. I know
roadrunners eat quail, but I don't think they're an important
factor. I think there wasn't any hatch. I don't know why."

Eben keeps diaries on "things that are going on" ecologically. These red-bound journals line his bookshelves, dating
back to 1958. "It might not matter if something happens two
or three years in a row," he says. "But over ten years, it
means something."

Driving toward town, we survey the naked, sculpted hills.
When I comment that the primary natural force they seem
to reflect is wind, Eben says that he attributes 75 percent of
their appearance to water, 15 percent to wind. Some 5 or 10
percent he ascribes to animals. "I've never known anyone in
geology who attributed much importance to the digging and
burrowing of surface mammals," he allows. To support his
theories, he is assembling about a dozen photographic slide
sequences on local ecological phenomena. One of them docu-
ments the gradual disappearance of a boulder in a cow pasture. Small animals burrow around the borders of the
boulder, creating a honeycomb in the ground underneath.
Cattle circulate around the rock, rubbing against it and
wearing a basin at the base. Rainwater collects in the basin
and, hence, the honeycomb — which turns to mud and
eventually collapses, sinking the rock. It has sunk ten inches
in the fifteen years that Eben has been photographing it.

"Once that rock is buried, geologists will tell you that it

happened in a flood," he says. "They like to think that things take hundreds of thousands of years. But I'm ready to argue that, in just a hundred and fifty years, animals can change the geological aspect of the surface."

Eben makes a brief stop at the Cholame post office, near the junction of California Highway 46 and the Palo Prieto Pass Road. Outside the post office is a mirrored monument bearing an inscription:

JAMES DEAN

1931 Feb 8 – 1955 Sept 30 5:59 ∞

"After he crashed, parts of his wreck were here for a couple or three weeks," says Eben. "People were flying in from all over. I never went down. Unless a man could help him, what was the use of seeing his wreck? People have these damn idols . . . he was a pretty good actor, I guess."

Near Shandon, a few miles farther west, Eben leaves the main highway in order to survey another subject of his slide shows. We stop at a bridge over the Estrella River, whose banks and bed are full of trees and shrubs. "When I was a kid, there were just a few trees and sterile sand here," Eben says. "Why do you think there are so many now? I'll give you a hint. Twenty years ago, nitrogen fertilizer began to be used heavily around here." He descends the riverbank and walks in the sand below the bridge. "The trees that grow up in this fertilized soil are catching more and more sand. When I started photographing this, the riverbed was fourteen feet below the bridge." Standing in the riverbed, Eben — five feet nine inches tall — now reaches up and easily touches the bottom of the bridge. "Every year, I put a black paintmark just above the water level, and every year after that, the mark is gone. Farmers in the last fifteen years have been mining the soil, not farming it. Most of the farms around here are on land that's so steep it shouldn't be plowed at all.

If you had a penny for every yard of topsoil that's gone down the Estrella and Salinas rivers just in the last five years, you wouldn't be able to count all your money if you lived to be a thousand. But you *will* live long enough to read that the Army Corps of Engineers is dredging the Salinas River to keep the town of Paso Robles from washing away. In fifty years, to save the towns along that river, the government will have to spend five dollars for every dollar the farmers ever made. The farmer will have lost all his topsoil by then, but the farmer doesn't know. The farmer doesn't know, and the farmer doesn't care."

In Paso Robles, we pull into a gas station to fill six cans with unleaded fuel. Eben gets out of the truck and a snarling dog lunges at him from the bed of a pickup parked at the next pump.

"There's an old hobo saying that you can tell a man by his dog," Eben says when he gets back into the cab. "If you were approaching a house for a meal and the dogs barked at you, you knew you might as well keep walking, because those kind of people would never give you a meal. Animals are like people; that there is just as if somebody walked by my car and my kid growled from the back, '*Hey, you son of a bitch, what're you doing!*' A pet you can't control isn't worth a damn. The first lesson I teach a horse or a dog is that they perform because I want them to, not because they want to. The secret of having a good animal is to keep him thinking all the time that if he doesn't follow your demands, all hell will break loose. All through the animal kingdom that psych system is at work. One guy will walk into a bar and just by his carriage send a message of respect to everybody in there. Another guy can be real blustery, but everybody'll laugh at him. This is why people have so much trouble with young children now — the children know the parents better than the parents know them. People say they don't want their children or their pets to be afraid of them, but it isn't fear — it's respect. A horse or dog doesn't give any more of a damn about you than it does about another dog or a post. When you lose respect, you lose it all."

The next stop is the supply store where Eben buys his chicken wire. In the store window is a poster that says *Make a Browning part of your family* over a picture of a gray-haired man with his hand on the shoulder of a boy who presumably is shooting a Browning rifle. Eben tells the young blond clerk that he wants to buy 250 feet of six-gauge galvanized annealed wire. The clerk leads him into the yard and starts twisting the wire from a spool. "It's fifty-five cents a pound," the kid says. "Five twists to the pound, five feet to the twist. So you need about ten pounds."

Eben says, "You've got a mathematical mind. You ought to be a banker."

The kid hands him the wire and asks, "That feel like about ten pounds?"

Eben hefts it. "Add three more twists," he says. Then, walking back into the store, he asks the clerk, "So, is it going to rain?"

"I don't know about *rain*," the kid answers. "Fog, maybe."

Eben says, "I live up in the Bitterwater country where I can look down on it. This morning the fog looked like you could walk on it." The clerk disappears and Eben confides, "I just ask about the weather to see if they're paying attention. He seems relatively sharp."

The clerk returns from the rear of the store. "You and I ought to go into business," he tells Eben. "That was ten pounds right on the nose."

It's getting hot. As we load the wire, I ask Eben if he knows a place where we might have a beer before heading back to the ranch. (Gladys allows no alcohol on the premises.) Eben drives to a low-slung bar, the Rodeo, across the street from a public park. There's a neon guitar and Budweiser sign in the window, and, inside, numerous boars' heads with protruding tusks menace customers from the wall. Nevertheless the place is packed, brimming with noon jollity. As we sit down, Eben remarks, "You've got to go into a bar to hear laughter nowadays. Time was when they'd call you a bum for being in a bar at this time of day."

"I agree," says a man on a stool beside us. "Anybody who would be in a bar at this time of day is definitely a bum."

Eben and I order a pair of drafts. The vocalizer next to us is wearing a mustache and a Mickey Mouse T-shirt. Smiling and somewhat overweight, he leans toward us, eager to socialize. In short order, he tells us that he has just returned to the United States after several years in Hong Kong.

"You guys really screwed up this country while I was away," he announces. "I can't believe the prices now. I had to buy some pants today. Guess how much it costs for a pair of blue jeans that say Sergio Valente on the ass?"

Eben says, "Well, I'm not sure, but I like to make a try at these things. Thirty-seven fifty."

"Sixty-two dollars. Unbelievable."

"In the early thirties, diesel gasoline cost four cents a gallon," says Eben. "I remember bargaining with people for cattle and trying to give them more than they were asking for the quality of what I was getting. They'd try to get me to pay them *less*. Storekeepers would carry people for a whole year, then give them a jackknife for paying off their bill."

"The fifties were the most prosperous time in U.S. history," the guy on the stool says.

"The fifties were when an honest dollar started to go down the drain," Eben answers. "After World War Two, making money became a sort of ritual or cult. You'd get on an airplane, and in the first-class compartment you'd see all these sharpies calculating their equations. Making *money* — not making a living. You could put a dollar down almost anywhere and it would turn into two or three."

Our companion lights a Kool. "This is the best time in U.S. history to be alive," he now says. "There are no wars; the standard of living is the highest it's ever been."

"Things are getting faster and faster all the time," Eben cautions.

"Good!" The guy smiles, leaning toward us again. "They're supposed to. *Some* inflation is healthy — four to six percent. You just have to control it."

Eben wraps his good hand around one of two beers that have just arrived. "You think the standard of living should just keep going up and up?"

"Definitely!" the guy sings, playing along. "Like a balloon!" He waves his cigarette in the air and grins.

Eben says, "The higher it goes, the farther it falls."

"Society has to progress. Otherwise you stagnate. That's why we aren't fish sitting here."

Eben studies the rows of beer cans behind the bar: Tecate, El Rancho, Grain Belt, Red Cap, Lone Star, North Star, Brown Derby, Iron City. "But eventually you get to where the environment will no longer support you," he says. "We're at the point now where, to enjoy the fruit of our labors, we have to make do with less."

The guy takes a swallow of beer and a pull on his cigarette. He regards Eben for a moment, then announces: "I've got ten acres over near Nacimiento."

"Whereabouts?"

"You swing north toward San Antonio by the Busy Bee market . . ."

"You mean Bee Rock?"

"Right. Actually, I haven't been able to find it. I bought it from a real estate agent up in Monterey. I couldn't get a mortgage without a house on it, so I spent all my savings on it, and now I can't afford to build a house. I'm gonna plant black walnuts — the government will give them to me."

"You ought to plant oaks," Eben suggests. "They're native to this country, resistant to every disease. It's good wood. You can sell it."

"All I know is that my grandfather made a lot of money on black walnut in New Hampshire. Ten acres isn't enough to make a living from, but it's enough to survive. I could have a garden and shoot a deer every once in a while."

Eben says, "If you've got enough to survive, that's making a living."

"We're talking about two different things."

Eben takes a drink, then rests his forearms on the bar. "What kind of work do you do?" he asks.

"I work for the Defense Department. I install computer systems for the army and navy." He looks at us, then looks away. "I don't always agree with what they do. If I could afford to get out, I would. But I can't."

"That's what John D. Rockefeller said," says Eben. "After he made his first fifty million, he couldn't afford to get out."

"My grandparents were truck farmers. I didn't want any part of that. I was wrong."

"When were you born?" Eben asks.

"Nineteen fifty-one."

"Is that right!" Eben exclaims. "I would've thought you were about fifteen years older than that."

"It's been a hard life."

"Married about three times?"

"Once. It didn't work."

"It shows," says Eben. "A man's maturity goes up with every marriage." He drains his draft. "I'm kind of interested in psychology," he says. "Why didn't your marriage work? Was it her voice, or the way she cooked, or what?"

"Personal stupidity," the guy says. "On my part. The

more women I meet, the more I see what a good woman she was."

"What's the old song?" says Eben. " 'A good woman is hard to find? ' "

"She won't take me back. I've written her letters."

"Well, that's interesting," says Eben. "It takes a gentleman to admit he made a mistake. Everybody has the right to one mistake. Just don't make another one."

Later, on the way home, Eben says, "I try to avoid bars, because you always get involved with a fella like that. They'll give anything a whirl — they're masters of the moment. Inside the bar they're real philosophers. Outside the bar you can't find them."

He continues driving, staring ahead, thinking about the interaction. Rare is the personal encounter from which Eben fails to draw some lesson.

"You know," he finally says, "young people are much more frank today. If you had asked an older person like myself about some of those things, they'd immediately throw up some kind of defense. At least he was willing to admit his mistakes. It shows that in some ways young people are a lot more objective today."

As we drive back through Shandon we hear a voice shout "Hey!" It's Eben's red-bearded son, Greg, wearing a red and white baseball hat, cutoff jeans, and a T-shirt that says STOP DIABLO CANYON BEFORE IT STOPS US. Eben slows to a stop and Greg approaches the truck.

"I saw my first young quail of the year today," Greg announces, grinning.

"Is that right," says Eben. "Where was it?"

"In a roadrunner's mouth."

"I'll be darned!"

Greg lives just over the hill from Eben, on land Eben deeded to him from his own ranch. To get there, Eben directs visitors "up past the chicken house and over by the windmill." The tail of Greg's windmill has a condor painted on it. His place is even more sun-baked — devoid of trees — than Eben's was forty years ago. To correct this problem, Greg plants fifteen fruit trees a year. In his future he envisions a livelihood based on the sale of sun-dried fruit. His house, which he built, is heated by passive solar conduction from a greenhouse; it obtains electricity from photovoltaic cells, and hot water from solar collector panels on the roof. Still, Greg says the most efficient solar collector he owns is his black Labrador retriever. He gets the dog to release its energy by making it run alongside his truck, but he hasn't yet figured out a way to harness the power. You get the impression that it's merely a matter of time.

Greg met his wife, Linda — a fourth-generation San Franciscan descended from West Africans and Iroquois Indians — on an Audubon lecture trip. Greg frequently gives talks and makes films for the Audubon Society, as Eben did until recently. For years Eben had an agreement with the San Luis Obispo Audubon chapter that he would serve as its president if nobody else was available. Since the national organization has joined forces with the U.S. Fish and Wildlife Service for the purpose of capturing condors, he has terminated his membership.

"The Audubon Society no longer represents its constituents," he explains. "It's become a bureaucracy. I tried to warn them against getting into a position where they couldn't oppose the Fish and Wildlife Service. Any organization, when it gets that big, has maintaining the organization as its primary goal; its philosophical purposes come second. The Audubon Society's board of directors is a group of big shots in New York — financiers, businessmen, banks. They don't know any more about what's going on out here than what goes on on the back side of the moon."

In his 1981 book, *John Muir and His Legacy: The American Conservation Movement*, Stephen Fox wrote: "The record of the National Audubon Society has been one of the singular mysteries of conservation history. After incorporation in 1905 it was usually the richest, most stable, potentially most useful of all conservation groups. Perhaps *too* stable . . . it raised money and maintained existing programs but seemed frozen in memories of the old battles . . . it still resisted the more activist impulses of the state societies, especially Massachusetts Audubon." Fox maintains that the driving force behind American environmentalism has been the tradition of the "radical amateur" — the nature-loving activist who, unbeholden to conservation or government agencies for a living, is free to urge high-principled action without regard for pragmatic constraint. "Professionals keep the movement organized," Fox wrote. "Amateurs keep it honest."

This tradition — of which Eben and Ian McMillan might be said to provide perfect examples — also spawned the Audubon Society. Founded in 1886 by George Bird Grinnell — editor and publisher of *Forest and Stream* magazine and cofounder (with Theodore Roosevelt) of the big-game conservationist Boone and Crockett Club — for the purpose of protecting wild birds and their eggs, the organization had a first-class pedigree from the outset, attracting a coterie of wealthy and distinguished members including Oliver Wendell Holmes and John Greenleaf Whittier. Despite this endowment, Grinnell (an amateur, after all) allowed the club to expire a few years after its inception; in 1896, however, it was revived in Massachusetts to protest the destruction of heron habitat in the South. Sixteen other state chapters quickly followed, their collective influence helping to pass the Lacey Act of 1900, which outlawed the interstate shipment of birds killed in violation of state laws and placed the ultimate responsibility for enforcement on the federal government. (Audubon members aided the cause by searching local markets for rare feathers in hats.) In 1905, the various state groups banded together to form the National Association of Audubon Societies.

Since then, the organization has grown to include some 500 local chapters and 500,000 members (between 1965 and 1975 alone, Audubon's membership increased by 800 percent, from 4,500 to 321,500) and has expanded its aims far beyond the original one to protect birds — it sponsors research, education, and political action on a broad range of environmental issues, publishes books and magazines, and raises funds for its $29 million annual budget through slick direct-mail campaigns. As this growth has taken place, Audubon and other successful environmental groups such as the Sierra Club and the Wilderness Society have outgrown their radical amateur origins to become professionally run organizations. They no longer recruit their directors from within the environmental movement but rather seek managerial candidates with strong financial and entrepreneurial backgrounds from business, industry, and government, paying them salaries as high as $100,000 a year. Former Audubon President Russell Peterson, for example, is also a former chairman of the board of the Du Pont corporation, a former Republican governor of Delaware, and a former chief of the Council on Environmental Quality under Presidents Nixon and Ford. This is not to imply that contradictions and conflicts of interest have developed only recently; from the beginning, Audubon was torn by internal disputes over its associations with sportsmen's organizations, gun companies, and the U.S. Fish and Wildlife Service, whose business — protecting game animals from habitat destruction — it shares.

The USFWS began life in 1886 — the same year as Audubon — as the Division of Economic Ornithology and Mammalogy in the U.S. Department of Agriculture. Its original purpose was to determine which animals were beneficial and which were detrimental to farmers; in attempting to carry out this aim, it began compiling a biological survey of the United States, and so was eventually renamed the Bureau of the Biological Survey. Pest control was a primary order of business from the beginning; in its first year of existence, the division tested poisons to stem the spread of the English sparrow, which (presaging the starling) was multiplying unchecked. Congress appropriated $125,000 for the Biological Survey to initiate predator control activities in 1915, and in 1931 it passed the Animal Damage Control Act, authorizing the agency to "eradicate, suppress, destroy or bring under control . . . mountain lions, wolves, coyotes, bobcats, prairie dogs, gophers, ground squirrels, jack rabbits, and other animals injurious to agriculture, horticulture, forestry, animal husbandry, wild game animals, furbearing animals, and birds." Today the Fish and Wildlife Service — as it was rechristened in 1940, when Franklin Roosevelt combined it with the Department of Commerce's Bureau of Fisheries, placing both in the Interior Department — is a 6,000-employee organization invested with a multitude of duties: enforcing fish and wildlife laws, managing animal refuges, protecting wildlife habitat, providing recreational fishing, conducting research, and — last but not least — preserving endangered species.

For the purpose of protecting condor habitat, Audubon and the Fish and Wildlife Service joined forces in 1964 to fight a proposed dam on Sespe Creek in Ventura County. (The project was eventually defeated in a public election by a margin of 36 votes.) They remained divided on the question of how best to preserve the condor population, however, until 1977. That year Audubon, which had previously lobbied against capturing condors, decided that the bird's plight was precarious enough to warrant drastic measures; the organization passed a resolution endorsing captive breeding, and a formal proposal was presented to Congress two years later. Accepted on February 26, 1980, the California Condor Recovery Plan was the first endangered species rescue program approved by the Fish and Wildlife Service since the passage of the Endangered Species Act of 1973.

When captive breeding was adopted as a course of action for condors, it wasn't a new idea. Egg transfers, the cross-fostering of young, artificial incubation and insemination had long been tools of zoos and the poultry industry; game birds and waterfowl had been propagated for release for many years, and aviculturalists and falconers had been breeding birds of prey for centuries. But the captive breeding and reintroduction of *endangered* species was something else again; in fact, not a single self-sustaining population of wild birds had yet resulted from the reintroduction of an endangered species into its original habitat. Problems with predators, tameness, and weather had resulted in widespread fatalities of Hawaiian geese, an oft-cited "success story." Whooping cranes had been bred in captivity with considerable fanfare, but none had been released; their eggs were successfully transferred to the nests of sandhill cranes, but to this day no transplanted whooping cranes have formed pair bonds or bred in the wild.* Successful introductions of birds have usually required repeated releases of large numbers, a luxury axiomatically unavailable to rare species. Typically, birds that have prospered after being released (starlings again leap to mind)

---

* On the other hand, the "natural" whooping crane population that migrates between Wood Buffalo National Park in Alberta and the Aransas National Wildlife Refuge in Texas increased from a low of fifteen in 1941 to ninety-six in 1986, solely through "conventional" conservation practices: protection of the habitat, education of hunters, and monitoring of the migratory route for pollution and disease.

possess three common characteristics: they have high reproductive rates; they're ecological "generalists" who can adapt
to many different environments; and they're gregarious (i.e.,
they form flocks), which allows them to find one another easily and mate.

Condors exhibit the opposite of each of these traits. The
reputed shyness or sensitivity of the species was one factor
that kept such groups as the Sierra Club, Friends of the
Earth, and some chapters of the Audubon Society from endorsing captive breeding. Although condors in flight often
seem curious about human beings — an attitude that has no
doubt contributed to the demise of the species — they are
notoriously skittish about nesting; they're known to have
abandoned nest sites within a half mile of hiking trails, and
Carl Koford observed that "one man can keep a pair of condors from the egg all night or prevent the feeding of a chick
for an entire day merely by exposing himself within 500
yards of the nest for a few minutes at one or two critical times
of day." Critics of the captive breeding plan wondered what
effect trapping would have on birds that got away; after
having a cannon net fired at them when they alighted at a
carcass, might they be reluctant to feed in the future? Given
that condors are highly dependent on learned behavior —
the young stay close to their parents for years following
birth — how would cage-raised birds learn to fend for themselves in the wild?

Some indications of answers to these questions were expected to be provided by Andean condors, which were already being bred in captivity by the USFWS at the Patuxent
Wildlife Research Center in Maryland. But in 1980, none of
the South American birds had yet been released to the wild.
Could we really afford to experiment, the environmentalists
asked, with the much more acutely endangered California
species? Wouldn't the money earmarked for captive breed-

ing — a total of $1 million from the two agencies involved, a figure that made this the most expensive endangered species preservation program ever undertaken — be better applied toward monitoring and maintaining the habitat? "If the Fish and Wildlife Service can take condors out of the wild and stick them in a zoo, why not do the same thing with wolves and bald eagles and allow drilling for oil in Alaska?" Sierra Club activist Mark Palmer asked during the condor hearings of 1980. His counterpart from Friends of the Earth, David Phillips, opined that "it's disgraceful for this to be the centerpiece of the government's endangered species program and for it to represent *habitat abandonment.*"

Contrary to the opinions of their critics, most endangered species biologists are aware that the central problem they face is endangered ecosystems. But the fact of the matter is that, however hard it may be to manipulate an endangered species, maintaining the animal's habitat is harder. Negotiating the bureaucratic maze of federal, state, and local governments, influencing and controlling private landowners, and resisting the relentless economic pressures of industry and development (not to mention identifying and eliminating the things that are killing the animals) are all necessary if threatened species' environments are to be preserved. Given the enormous difficulty and slowness of this task, practitioners of "clinical ornithology" (as the techniques of manipulative management have been termed) argue that, unless artificial aids are imposed, some endangered species will undoubtedly expire before their habitats are saved — if indeed they can be saved at all.

To this end, the proponents of captive propagation see their critics as shortsighted. As it happens, that's also how their critics see them and their quick-"fix" approach to the symptoms of the problem. "Premature and utterly out of balance" was how David R. Brower described the captive breeding proposal at the Santa Barbara hearing I attended.

Brower, America's most famous environmentalist, declared that "the condor is not an electronic toy to play with, rough up, manipulate, blindfold, manhandle, peer into, wire for sound, tinker with the great wings of, double-clutch, or put on crutches or behind bars," concluding that "the wilderness within the condor and the wilderness essential to it have rights. We deplore the overcuriosity of biologists who would invade that privacy." If land is viewed as a community (as Aldo Leopold recommended and as the environmentalists tend to view it), then taking condors into captivity for their own protection is no less outlandish a proposition than rounding up innocent citizens from dangerous neighborhoods and putting them in jail. In this view — which Eben and Ian McMillan share — an animal is first and foremost an expression of its ecosystem; removed from its natural habitat, it literally ceases to be that animal — it is merely a collection of genes in a cage.

This is the so-called mystical attitude with which the captive breeding scientists exhibit so little patience. "The definition of a condor is genetic, unless you've got several generations removed from the wild," Noel Snyder, the USFWS condor biologist, told me during a break in the round-table discussion at which I first met Eben. Snyder called the captive breeding critics "hopelessly impractical. They aren't dealing with the problem logically. They come in with this holier-than-thou attitude and don't even know what they're talking about."

The captive breeding debate, it seemed to me, was essentially one between modernists and fundamentalists. On the latter side were the radical amateurs, the Browers and the McMillans: distrustful of their own species' instincts, of artificial management, of technology itself with the price it had already extracted from the environment. On the other were the professionals — the powers that be: the American Ornithologists Union, the New York Zoological Society, the

World Wildlife Fund, the American Museum of Natural History, and the United States government — man applying the most spectacular emblem of his evolution (technology) to the animal that most spectacularly illustrates the expense at which he has evolved (the condor). There seemed to me something contradictory about this second position, something that smacked of the hubris associated with the condor's decline. Given that the federal agency responsible for preserving this scavenger was also spending $6 million a year poisoning predators (an apparent conflict of interest that was neatly illustrated in 1983, when a condor was killed by a cyanide trap that the USFWS had set out for coyotes), the program reminded me of the government's proclivity for pouring aid into countries it has just decimated.* The Fish and Wildlife Service was largely responsible for the extermination of the wolf throughout the continental United States; it brought the black-footed ferret to the verge of extinction through the poisoning of the prairie dog. While it seemed ironic that groups like the Audubon Society, the Sierra Club, and Friends of the Earth — which all ostensibly exist for the same purpose — couldn't agree on what their purposes were, the argument between the environmentalists and the U.S. Fish and Wildlife Service was far from ironic. As an agency of the federal government, the USFWS is axiomatically committed to the service of man — which, in its own ironic way, frequently excludes it from alignment with friends of the earth.

Eben says that his primary goal in his Audubon lectures was "to instill a sense of responsibility" in the people who listened to him. If the reader is yet unaware, Eben is big on re-

* This contradiction was erased — at least within the jurisdiction of the Fish and Wildlife Service — in late 1985, when Congress transferred federal responsibility for predator control back to the Department of Agriculture.

sponsibility. He once told me that he doesn't consider himself a nature lover: "It's not a matter of *enjoying* nature," he said. "It's a matter of being knowledgeable and responsible about your place." Eben thinks that "computers are taking away from us the responsibility of managing our own affairs" and that "all the schools are teaching privilege, but none are teaching responsibility." If cancer were cured, he theorizes, the average human life expectancy might rise by five years and "the average person would take that advantage, but wouldn't take the responsibility that went with it." To him, the highly symbolic condor is mainly a symbol of "the dereliction of environmental responsibility." When Eben studies birds, he doesn't band them: "Although they say it doesn't do them any harm, I can't help but think it's detrimental. Some call it animal rights, but I think of it as human responsibility — to be as little of an influence as possible." Of Los Angeles, a city he's forced to visit now and then, Eben says, "I can't think of any environment with less respect for or responsibility to any sort of creed." One time, after he and I had gone bird-watching with some people from L.A., one of whom had left his wife for a college student who subsequently left him, I asked Eben how he and Gladys had coped with extramarital distraction in fifty years of marriage. "Gladys and I are the same sort of person," Eben answered. "You'd never let it enter your mind not to be true to your responsibilities."

Gladys, who is partial to blue sneakers and cardigans, the sleeves of which she pushes up to the elbows, is, as might be expected of someone married to Eben, quiet. She could have been a terrific librarian, as she is also a tireless archivist. Among the weaker links in Eben's oratory is his memory for dates; when he holds forth, Gladys keeps mum, but if a question of chronology arises, she leaps into the limelight. Once, during dinner, Eben was trying to remember the year that he'd fallen from a horse and broken his knee. Gladys silently slipped toward the bookshelves. After a few minutes — during which Eben had given up — Gladys returned to the table and announced that the date of the fracture had been August 2, 1960. In her hands she held a red-bound diary. "You were on crutches for my father's funeral," she told Eben. "You had the cast taken off the day after May and Ian's daughter got married. I just started putting things together."

Gladys's pink and healthy-looking skin is furrowed with lines that encircle her face like an ad for the beauty of contour plowing. Her family came to California from Missouri during the Depression; her father, who had eight children, worked on ranches. So did Gladys, as a cook. So did Eben, as a cowboy. His skill with animals was renowned — his brother Don once told me that "with one hand, Eb was the greatest horseman of us all. He could hit a horse in the face and the next day it would walk right up to him. If I'd done that, I never would have seen the animal again."

"I was a good rider and roper," Eben admits. "I wasn't too cautious. In order to have the respect and admiration of your peers, you had to cultivate a devil-may-care attitude. Women would watch me breaking colts and say, 'What do you do that for? You're crazy.' " As it happened, Eben was breaking colts on a ranch where Gladys turned out meals every day at six A.M., noon, and six P.M. "Her efficiency was appealing," says Eben. "You didn't see too many young women except at a dance or something like that. Young people in those days were shy; it served as a safeguard against a plethora of breeding. Gladys was a nice-looking girl. After a while I decided I didn't want to be a bachelor any longer, so I courted her. We got married, and I made a run at getting established as a responsible citizen.

"I'd like to think that I was shopping responsibly and made a wise decision.

"Unlike that guy in the bar."

JOHN TAFT IS the president of the Conservation Endowment
Fund. I met him in the spring of 1983 when I went to hear
Eben give a talk in Ojai, a pleasant, moderately sized town
in the Santa Ynez Mountains northwest of Los Angeles. Development in southern Ventura County could be said to epit-
omize land trends responsible for the decline of condors.
After its settlement by the Spanish, the area was largely covered by the De La Guerra grant, upon which livestock grazed
almost all the way from the San Fernando Valley to the Pacific Ocean. In the 1880s this became the Las Posas Ranch,
home to some 60,000 sheep — a veritable cornucopia for
condors. But with the twentieth century and the explosion of
L.A., the Las Posas Ranch was subdivided; the better lands
were devoted to grains, then beans, then orchards. Today the
orchards are being replaced by houses, and condors have
long since disappeared.

Taft was building an octagonal house outside Ojai, on top of a hill in the Santa Ana River watershed. To reach the place, I drove through an oak forest and crossed a river, passed a bathing pool surrounded by simulated Indian petroglyphs, and knocked on the door of a stone house. A Mexican woman came to the door and ushered me inside. The pine walls of the house were decorated with the head of a buck and a print of a European moor hen. I was led to the kitchen, where Taft — a tall, rawboned man with square, senatorial features — was eating scrambled eggs and tortillas. He was wearing a hooded orange Mexican shirt over a navy blue undershirt. When he spoke to his employees in Spanish, his voice was deep and dramatic. Taft looked younger than I had anticipated after hearing this voice on the telephone. He had reddish sideburns, light freckles, and pale, translucent skin. His hair was gray at the temples — prematurely, it seemed, though he was in fact forty-eight.

We went out onto the back porch, which looked out over the alders in the river canyon. Taft said that on this site — or, rather, on the site of the octagonal house, a short distance uphill through the forest — he was going to start a center for "environmental awareness," an attribute that he said had been instilled in him by Eben McMillan.

"I met Eben in 1952, when I was eighteen years old," Taft said, gazing out over the canyon. "I went on an Audubon trip to Carneros Rocks, and there was Eben with little Gregory. I fastened onto him instantly. He saw my cameras — I'd been making movies since I was thirteen — and was impressed; later he invited me to his house to show a film I'd made called *The Return of Spring*. At that time they were living in this little tiny place about twenty feet square. I got there after dark. The kids were all around, and I was greeted royally, like a traveler from a distant land. It was a great feeling — one I never had before or since.

"I showed the film, and Eben immediately said, 'Let's make a film about this country here.' He didn't know anything about filmmaking, but the next day we drove around looking at eagles' nests and overgrazed slopes. It was the first time I'd ever seen the landscape in terms of man's use of it. I started going back there every week. I was working for my father, selling appliances, but for years and years, every Friday I'd leave here at three in the afternoon and get up to Eben's about six. During the week Eben would find things to film — larkspur, wasps' nests, prairie falcons, whatever — and I'd do the photography. Saturday night we'd look at film from the week before.

"There was a constant stream of people coming and going — naturalists, museum people, fish and game wardens, scientific people from the university. Eben would take them on trips around the countryside. Everyone was treated like somebody special — everything was dropped, and the visitor became the focus. If somebody wanted to see a plant, we'd drive down to the Carrisa Plains; if somebody wanted to look at bats, Eben knew where all the bat caves were. We'd pop up at six A.M., no matter what time we'd gone to sleep. I'd always hear Gladys scrubbing and cleaning the floors after we went to bed. In the morning, Eben would have a couple of letters written before anybody else was up. As soon as it got gray, we'd take a walk."

Eventually Taft and Eben formed a company called Environmental Films. In all, they made five movies: *The Shandon Hills, Land That I Love, Our Endangered Environment, The Central California Coastal Plain,* and *Yosemite: An Ecological Visit.*

"Eben wrote the scripts," Taft said. "He left most of the photography to me. I built an editing room near here, on Sulphur Mountain. Eben came down, and pretty soon he was telling me things about the place that I never knew existed. He became my mentor — a mentor in the true sense, of being nonjudgmental. He always put things to me in the form of questions. I didn't know birds at all in those days; I was interested in hawks and owls, but I didn't know an oriole from a red-winged blackbird. Eben would see a towhee and say, 'You suppose that's a sage thrasher, John?' I'd have to look at it and start thinking. If he'd just told me, I wouldn't have known the difference.

"One of the most important things Eben taught me was to be able to see *delicate* beauty. I could see beauty in a sunset, but it was Eben who showed me the small, intimate forms. I remember the day it first happened — we were in the San Juan Mountains photographing nighthawks. I turned around, and Eben had his back to me; he had his thirty-five-millimeter camera and was moving the viewfinder around. I asked him what he was photographing, and he said, 'These oats. Aren't they nice?' I didn't understand how anybody could see beauty in grass, but I focused my eyes on the fine lines of those oats, and I was amazed. My family never even had flowers in the house. They were the total opposite of the McMillans. We came from pioneer stock too, but where we sat down to meals of meat and gravy and vegetables, the McMillans would just have a bowl of potato soup. Their aim was to see how little you could get by on. There were never enough covers on my bed up there; all night long I'd be freezing to death. But for some reason I never hauled a blanket up there with me. I had read Thoreau, and the simple, frugal life was something to be looked up to.

"Eben set a marvelous example, but I was disappointed by him occasionally. When I first met him, he would shoot any bobcat that came in the yard — everything was for the quail. Now he's become totally tolerant. If he sees a sick animal, he might say, 'The poor devil,' where before he'd just say, 'Let nature take care of it.' He never showed compassion that way — not to his family, not to a dog. When we'd go somewhere in a car, he'd make the dog run for miles to exercise it. One time there was a fight, and I was horrified that Eben could smash a man in the face and knock him down when we were always condemning human beings for not controlling themselves. Eben would criticize his neighbors for taking government property while he was literally living off the Soil Bank. He concentrated on the faults in society without seeing the good points. Especially in rich men. You know, John D. Rockefeller gave a Yosemite redwood grove to society, but Eben would just say he was giving it back to the people he stole it from. I build trailer parks and shopping centers for a living; I decided that if I'm gonna have a job, I want to make a lot of dough and use it for conservationist purposes."

Taft paused to listen to the forest. "Do you hear that canyon wren?" he asked. "That's the most exciting thing my body will experience today. If all the things I've learned from Eben vanished from my mind, I'd be a mental pauper. He gave me the desire to know nature. He gave me the key. The *door* was there, but I needed the key. Ever since I opened that door, my life has been a marvelous event."

DURING DINNER, two deer are sighted in the wheat field to the north. "Deer can be quite a nuisance," says Eben. "They carry ticks that get on cattle, and they knock down quite a bit of grain. There didn't used to be too many around here, but when people started using secondary poisons like 1080 to get rid of coyotes, it allowed the deer to increase. For years you wouldn't see or hear a single coyote, and deer moved out into areas where they had never appeared before.

"I think it's predation of coyotes on fawns that controls deer. When deer get too plentiful they develop maladies, and a coyote can recognize them as prey long before a human can. Like mountain lions: these darn fools just lifted the moratorium because they say mountain lions decimate the deer herds. It's true you won't see many deer in lion country; they've always been a factor in controlling deer populations.

But not to the extent of man! Lions decimate the *excess* of deer; they're a leavening factor that keeps deer from being a problem in the natural environment. People don't even kill the sick ones; they want a big strong buck with a big set of antlers. What hunter would want to come dragging a poor old doe into town?"

The mountain lion — *Felis concolor,* which is also known as thc cougar, puma, panther, and "catamount" (a nickname I have never heard spoken, but which seems irresistible to every writer on the subject) — was, until recently, protected by a moratorium on sport hunting of the species in California, the only state to have taken such protective action. The puma was once the most widely distributed land mammal in the New World — it was found in deserts, jungles, mountains, and prairies from Patagonia to the Yukon (which also happens to be the original range of deer species in the Western Hemisphere) and used to inhabit every one of the United States. But as the North American white-tailed deer herd declined — from an estimated 43 million at the time of Columbus's arrival to around 300,000 in 1890 — the big cats disappeared as well. They are now known to exist only in the West, except for a few populations totaling perhaps 20 in the region of the Florida Everglades, with occasional unconfirmed sightings in places like Maine and even New York and New Jersey.

The consummation of carnivore evolution, pumas are highly skilled killers; in addition to venison, their diet has been shown to include skunk, porcupine, beaver, coyote, fox, rabbit, marmot, and mouse. Cats have never matched the depradatory impact that canines exert on commercial livestock, but cougars do take the odd sheep, calf, or colt; and for that reason (in concert with the old bugaboo of frontier paranoia, even though lion-inflicted deaths on North American humans can be counted on the fingers of one and a half

Homo sapiens hands) they were hunted mercilessly throughout the West until very recently — states paid bounties of up to $100 for every dead cat. California once employed five professional lion hunters, and between 1908 and 1963 the state paid out 12,500 lion bounties.

One of the last of these killings occurred in Big Sur, claiming a cougar that had been a favorite of Margaret Owings — local resident, conservationist, wife of a nationally known architect, and Ian McMillan's predecessor on the state parks commission. When Mrs. Owings — whom some credit with the achievement of singlehandedly saving the southern sea otter — learned that her favorite cat had been killed for $100, she and Ian began lobbying the state legislature to eliminate puma bounties. In 1969 the lion was reclassified in California from "vermin" to "game," subject to hunting restrictions imposed by the state fish and game department; three years later a coalition of conservationists, fearing that the species might be endangered, won a four-year moratorium on lion hunting. The ban was extended in 1976, 1980, and 1984, and passed the state legislature again in 1986. But — despite an endorsement from the California Cattleman's Association and severe compromises in the bill, which essentially ended up recommending only that the lion population be studied — it was vetoed by Governor George Deukmejian, who maintained that it was "unnecessary to statutorily treat the mountain lion differently from other game animals." At this writing, the species is again considered fair game throughout the American West, where the number of cougars killed has increased by 50 percent in the past decade.

One reason for lifting the hunting ban — as was urged by the National Rifle Association and the California Wildlife Federation (a sport-hunting organization whose former president, a gunstore owner named Howard Carper, had been forced by conservationist pressure to resign as director of the state fish and game department after being appointed to the post by Deukmejian) — was the theory that lions had proliferated since its imposition. In 1972, the first year of the moratorium, 5 livestock killings were attributed to cougars in California; by 1985 the number had risen to 138 (though this figure may reflect the fact that ranchers now document such incidents, whereas they once went unreported). In 1984 it was estimated that there were some 4,800 cougars in the state, plus or minus 700 — a guess based on the assumption that lions had been increasing by 8 percent per year since the hunting ban was imposed. The population estimate in 1972 had been only half that — 2,400, subjectively arrived at by dividing the amount of "suitable lion habitat" in the state by the typical size of a puma's territory. In 1976, Carl Koford had come up with an even lower figure — 1,000 — by counting cougar tracks on backcountry roads, and during the sixties the New York Zoological Society had estimated that there were only 4,000 to 6,500 lions left in the entire West.

In fact, nobody knows how many mountain lions there are in California or anywhere else — or whether the numbers are growing or shrinking — because the animal is the most secretive and elusive creature in all of North America. Even when a puma reveals itself — a rare occurrence — its long, low, earth-colored torso is exceedingly difficult to spot; scientists who study lions rarely see their subjects, following them rather by their radio collars, which can only be attached after hounds have found and treed the cats. In eighty years of life in the open, Eben McMillan has seen a mountain lion once.

"I was on a bulldozed fire trail in the Santa Lucias, looking for wild cattle," says Eben. "I came around a rock, and by golly there was this lion, half sitting, no more than thirty yards away. He looked at me with this benevolent grin — as if a wild animal could smile, and he might have said, 'Why hello, fella, good morning!' Just sort of a friendly guy. Then in about one, two, three, four seconds" — Eben ticks them off with his index finger — "he turned around and went down on his belly and his shoulder blades went way up high behind him and he went over the bulldozer berm just like a snake. He was more liquid than animal — I never saw his feet move. He just dipped his head down and got his throat right down along the ground and gave you the impression that he was just a part of the earth.

"All my life I've conditioned myself to see as much as I could at first glance, but this lion kind of overwhelmed me. The thing that impressed me most was the size of that devil's tail. It was as big around as my calf — not tawny yellow, more gray-brown. I've seen grizzly bear and moose, but nothing else ever impressed me the way that mountain lion did. My God, it was a beautiful big animal! It was a great experience."

IT IS EARLY in the morning and we are near the top of a mountain. Along the shoulders of the road, hunters appear and disappear; their fluorescent orange hats and coats take shape and then diminish in the fog, the visual equivalent of clanging buoys. Visibility perhaps extends to 100 feet. Rain and wind have drawn a maze of channels on the windshield of the pickup, although it is September — officially too early for rain in California. Nevertheless, water falling from the sky is beating a steady snare-drum roll on the camper top. I sit under it in the back, bouncing on the tire wells with Eben; we face each other across a chilly atmosphere that makes faint clouds of our breath.

The truck is climbing a badly rutted dirt road toward the summit. Granite extrusions and Ponderosa pines pass within a foot of the windows. Eben stares out at them as he rocks from side to side, gripping the edges of his ridged steel seat. He wears a bent gray felt cowboy hat and a navy blue windbreaker. In the early light his eyes seem as cold as the air; when Eben takes his glasses off and isn't squinting in the sun, his eyes reveal their true color, which is the color of ice.

On top of the mountain, seven cars sit facing a billboard in a full-bore gale. Rain comes in horizontally up here; we get out of the truck, and I have to pull my hat low on my head to prevent it from flying away. Just downhill, a park ranger is pulling a gigantic pump hose toward an outhouse from a light green truck. Thoroughly soaked, he smiles up at us. The pines around him are whitebark and Jeffrey; lightning has transformed the trunk of one into an upside-down U, but the tree is still living.

The billboard says:

The California condor, a rare and endangered species fully protected by state law, can be seen from this point. Adult birds may be identified by their large size, black color with orange head, and by the triangular white patch on the underside of each wing. The condor has an average wingspread of nine feet, the longest of any North American land bird. Riding favorable air currents, it can soar and glide for more than one hour at a time in steady flight. From June through October one or more condors may usually be seen soaring in the vicinity of this observation site. Help protect and preserve this vanishing species.

Los Padres National Forest
U.S. Department of Agriculture

On clear days, the view from this spot encompasses great vistas of brown cliffs, blue ridges bordering the Cuyama River, and the multicolored patchwork of farms in the San Joaquin Valley. Today the view is about what you'd get from inside an oxygen tent. Nevertheless, Eben insists on walking the narrow trail to the lookout to make sure that no one from our proposed party is out there looking for condors. "They'd have to be crazy to be out there," he allows, "but birders are crazy."

The path to the lookout is covered with asphalt and lined with granite rocks. No one — not even a birder — is out there. We return to the parking lot, and Eben confers with several of the people sitting in the cars. Satisfied that we've found everyone we're going to find, he climbs back into the truck; this time we ride in front, with heat and other humans, back down the mountain to a wide place in the road, which Eben has designated as a meeting spot.

The mountain is Mount Pinos — at 9,000 feet, the highest peak in the Tehachapis. If you look at the major mountain ranges of California on a map, they form a kind of horseshoe: the open end of the shoe is in the north; the eastern prong is the Sierra Nevada; the Coast Ranges constitute the wing to the west. The southern segment of the shoe — the part you might grip if you aimed to pitch all these mountains toward a stake somewhere in, say, the USSR — is made up of the Transverse Ranges (including the Tehachapis), which run east-west 60 miles north of the Los Angeles basin. To some ways of thinking, these mountains are the true barrier between northern and southern California: dry, rugged country of sandstone and chaparral, where timeworn cliffs loom like parapets in a Pleistocene animal's Alamo — the last refuge of the California condor.

Once a year, Eben leads a condor watch for the National Audubon Society's Golden Gate chapter (one that has broken with the organization's leadership and rejected captive breeding). The traditional site for the event is Mount Pinos and the traditional time is late September — calving season on the cattle ranches in the foothills of the Tehachapis. Many of the calves are stillborn, and about one cow in ten will fail to survive the ordeal of childbirth; the result on enormous grazing tracts like the Hudson, Snedden, and San Emidio ranches (especially when combined with the effects of the first week of deer hunting season) is a landscape littered with carcasses and afterbirth — and, as a consequence, condors.

I had driven down the previous day with Eric Caine, a strong, nervous, thirty-fivish fellow with a mustache and maniacal laugh whom I'd met in August at a condor hearing before the state fish and game commission. When he picked me up, Caine was wearing a felt hat, a leather vest, a checked shirt, and camouflage sneakers. In the three-piece suit that he'd worn to the hearing in Sacramento, Caine had looked like a Sierra Club lawyer; in fact, he was a Modesto shoestore manager with a consuming interest in California condors. As we drove south in the San Joaquin Valley, he told me that he'd gotten interested in ornithology a few years before on a trip to Sequoia National Park, where he'd run into an old high school friend who was there looking at birds.

"I took it as a sure sign that domestic life had corrupted him," Caine said. "But he handed me the binoculars; I saw a redbreasted nuthatch, and it was just stunning. Later, at home, I saw some egrets and realized that this was a part of the world I knew nothing about. So I bought some binoculars and started doing a lot of reading. I began accumulating species for a life list, and one bird I needed was a California condor."

In August of 1979, Caine saw that Golden Gate Audubon was sponsoring a field trip to Mount Pinos led by Carl Koford. "I drove down there, and when I got to the parking lot, here was this scraggly old guy in a pickup who said he was going to lead the trip because Koford was sick. It was Eben McMillan. I was pretty disappointed that Koford wasn't there, and as the day went on I began to think that Eben was a man with a severe drinking problem. You know how he tends to ramble. It got to be about two o'clock in the afternoon and everybody was falling asleep when all of a sudden Eben yelled, 'Five condor!' They came right over the mountain within forty yards of us. It was a tremendous experience. There's something about the way a condor flies that's fascinating to me; I never get tired of looking at them. When you're all by yourself in a remote place and you see a condor, it's a little bit scary. There's an intake of breath; there's awe involved. It has the rudiments of a religious experience. It's such a big metaphor for life on earth. There's just a magnetism about it."

Nine months later, Caine read in the newspaper about the wild condor chick that died from shock at being handled by the captive breeding biologists. Impulsively, he called Eben, and pretty soon the two of them were going birding together. Eric had since changed his opinion of Eben to the point where he called him "a hero. He's physically strong, morally committed, free. He gets beat, but he never gets defeated." Eric himself had taken to writing letters and testifying before the Fish and Game Commission (at the hearing where I met him, he'd proffered an empty shotgun shell that he'd found near the condor sanctuary), and now, he said, he often drove down to Mount Pinos for a day to "fool around, talk to people, sleep on hillsides." In fact, he had become something of an authority on the California condor.

"Before I got involved with the condor, I didn't have a focus in my life," Eric explained. "I'd gotten into grad school in rhetoric but decided not to go. I was burned out. I'm an alcoholic — I had quit drinking, but I had a blood sugar problem, and I was depressed about not going to grad school. Somebody offered me a job managing a shoestore, so I took it.

"Every day, my job is to do more business than the store

did a year ago. A guy like me, in the nine-to-five world, needs a cause higher than scrambling for a buck. Birds and nature have become my major source of serenity in life. There are a lot of things I believe in now — things that seem to be un-questionably right. There's no vacillation, no argument about whether it's right to preserve nature, peace, and beauty."

Eben was animated when we picked him up. Field trips tend to get him excited. As we drove southwest through Choice Valley and Blackwell's Corner, his conversation with Caine was energetic; Eben punctuated Eric's rap with frequent by-gollies and I'll-be-darneds, or, when those were exhausted, simple ohs and ahs. Eben reported that he and Gladys had just returned from the Pacific Northwest, where forests that had been closed due to fire hazard had been opened briefly so that jobless loggers could salvage dead timber before it rotted.

"Boy!" said Eben. "When they turned those loggers loose, it was just like an ant den that you'd stepped in. The trucks were roaring all night long; the bars were full of people spending money instead of saving it for when the boom ended."

Eric said, "It's because they don't have any faith in the fu-ture."

"Is it because they have no faith in the future, Eric?" Eben asked. "Or is it because they just don't think? I've gotten to where I believe constructive thinking is about as far from the average American as we are from the South Pole."

It was a gray, dank day that made the barren brown early autumn landscape seem oppressive — even emptier than usual. As we traveled through it, the normal complement of natural phenomena was performed by the local fauna. A golden eagle tearing at a squirrel carcass on the side of the road allowed the car to come unusually close, then took off and flew alongside us, its huge wings flapping just feet from the car. "This time of year you see things like that," Eben said. "The mammals go underground and the migrating eagles get pretty hungry." Farther on, an enormous fuzzy spot was crossing the road — a tarantula, as it turned out. Eben: "They claim that the ones we see are more than twenty years old. They're looking for a female and that's why they're out traveling. This is a high-mortality time of year for them. The pepsis wasp is a leavening factor on spider populations. They call it the tarantula hawk — it paralyzes the tarantula, then lays its eggs on it. The larvae tunnel inside and develop there. There are hundreds of different kinds of pepsis wasps, and each one uses a different spider."

It started to rain. The road ran straight as pencil lead through a sandy landscape filled with oil pumps. Kern County, California, happens to be the nation's fourth (after Texas, Alaska, and Louisiana) and the world's eighteenth (after countries including Ecuador, Gabon, and Qatar) largest oil-producing region. Some four million barrels of crude are pumped from it every week, and to drive through its midsection, on Highway 33 west of Bakersfield, is to be enveloped by the viscera of the petrochemical industry. The earth appeared to have been wholly occupied in the pursuit of oil; the pumps extended as far as the eye could see. There were oil pumps in parking lots; there were oil pumps in the backyards of houses where oil workers lived. Where there weren't oil pumps, there were tanks — beige pillboxes linked by a legion of red and yellow pipes. The pumps were black, with red letters — 677HR, 428BL. The air above them was filled with power lines and the odor of petroleum. The ground was crisscrossed by dirt tracks leading into the sagebrush — access roads carved from ashen earth. At the head of each was a lease sign for Getty, Chevron, or Mobil. Later,

I learned that one of the fields we passed through had been purchased by Shell for the tidy sum of $3,653,272,000.

"This country used to be sagebrush," Eben said, gazing out the window. Then, in a sudden fit, he blurted, "Goldang it, they're taking all this money and perverting our society! The oil companies probably spent thirty-five or forty thousand dollars on the Kern County supervisor race. The numskulls they elect aren't in there because of any managing ability or wisdom — they're in there because they'll do what the oil companies want them to do."

At a tiny crossroads called Derby Acres, we passed a grocery (BEER AND POP) with its windows boarded up but a sign that said OPEN — the sort of anomalous sight that attends civilization in both the desert and the inner city. Here the reason for the plywood was wind, which in summer sends sand across the sagebrush-less landscape, obscuring visibility to such an extent that occasional twelve-car pileups are created. When United Artists Studios needed to simulate Pampa, Texas — the Dust Bowl town where Woody Guthrie grew up — for the movie *Bound for Glory,* this was where they came. At Taft, the largest town in the area, with a population of 15,000, the streets were lined with California fan palms. Taft is the site of Oildorado, an annual festival that features, among other things, world championships in welding and backhoe racing. Contestants for the title of Oildorado Queen wear signs that say MAID OF PETROLEUM. Taft has an oil museum, and the hills outside town are dotted with wooden derricks — antiques from the beginning of the region's petroleum era, which was pinpointed by a state historical landmark sign:

First Gusher
1909
Midway Field
6 Miles

Driving past it, I realized that California's oil age is two years younger than Eben.

On the far side of Taft, Eric pulled over and stopped the car in a dirt lot by the highway. Eben had mentioned that this place had "a good view," and indeed it did have an excellent view of trucks — a steady stream of them downshifting noisily, preparing to climb the grade outside town. Our sandlot seemed to serve mainly as a place for drivers to sleep, and this was apparently what Eben and Eric had done one evening the previous year. In the middle of the night, Eric had awakened to see one of the rarest and most delicate mammals of North America regarding him at close range.

"It was a full moon," Eric remembered. "There was light enough to read by. It was the time of the summer star showers from Perseus; I'd been watching them and dozed off. When I woke up, there was a kit fox three feet away. I thought I was dreaming, so I said to myself, Well, I'll sit up and see what happens. He backed up a couple of feet and continued looking at me. There was no sign of fear at all — there was nothing furtive about him. He went and sniffed Eben's sleeping bag up and down twice; he went over the whole place like a Geiger counter. His intelligence was obviously olfactory — you could almost see the stream of information going through his nose. He didn't so much move from place to place as reappear in different spots; he was just like a little wisp of smoke, a few bits of fur held together by piano wire. There was no excess on him. You could see he was made to survive in rough places. I watched him for three or four minutes until he walked away. It was one of the real experiences of my life." Now Eben and Eric were making what amounted to a pilgrimage, walking around in the rain by a roaring highway in the middle of thousands of oil wells, searching for signs of an endangered species — and finding nothing but empty shotgun shells.

"He wouldn't have much of a chance here," Eben admitted, filling his pockets with the spent shells. Then he leaned over to poke apart a small pile of scat with a stick. After studying it for a few seconds, he raised himself up and proclaimed it the feces of a kit fox. He and Eric seemed genuinely gratified, and we got back in the car and drove on.

Later, Eben told me that the scat was "just as identifiable as if a car went by that was a Cadillac or a Ford. There were at least a dozen factors to judge from: the size, the composition, the relation to other droppings that were there. There was probably a year's worth, at two-month intervals. There was microtine rodent fur in it, so it had to be a predator. It wasn't a cat and it wasn't a weasel, so it had to be a small fox. At this time of year it wouldn't be a young fox, so it must have been a kit fox."

And the mortality factors? The shotgun shells and the traffic?

"The shells were probably diurnal. Being close to the road would discourage species that might compete with it. I've noticed that foxes live along roads; it could be that they're clever enough to negotiate the lights and the traffic patterns. You find kit fox around water holes, alluvial washes, the edges of trails; they don't like tall grass, they need visibility to hunt. There always have been kit fox in those bare hills, and I think there always will be."

The highway lost its straightness now, bending into big curves as it climbed through humped yellow hills of increasing steepness. I noted the onset of the dizzy euphoria that accompanies entry into foothills. To the west, the craggy ridges of the Caliente Mountains seemed to be stacked on top of one another, receding into the distance under a low, dark gray sky that matched the color of the road. We passed a ranch house and Eben said, "This here's the guy who has a fence built of beer bottles. Now I see he's got an agricultural cooking machine. You've got to wonder what goes through the mind of a person like that." A little farther on we saw a big brown and white billy goat grazing untethered on a hillside, its lead rope dragging in the grass between its legs, and Eben insisted on stopping; he seemed astonished. "Boy, he's big! Fat! He's got balls on him just like old folks'." He left the car, cupped his hands by his mouth, and addressed the animal with sophisticated herding commands: "Hey! Hoo! *Vamos!*" The goat fixed us with something like contempt (its white beard suggesting a certain seniority) and moved off at a pace that was decidedly its own.

Eric said, "Eben, I talked to John Ogden, and he told me they've been finding strychnine containers."

"I'll be darned."

"They won't tell me where, but I bet it's here on the Hudson Ranch."

"These fellas always were worried about predators," said Eben.

The huge crescent formed by the Hudson, Santiago, and San Emidio ranches constitutes one of the biggest continuous cattle ranges in California. In February of 1980, however, the Hudson family sold their spread of over 11,000 acres to a group of investors headed by one Richard Hadley, a Seattle shipping magnate. His plan was to develop the property according to an "agrominium" (i.e., agricultural condominium) concept: there would be seven hundred homes in clusters, a rodeo complex, a system of horse trails, and some bona fide agricultural uses (possibly the planting of vineyards) to be owned in common by the homebuyers.

Unfortunately, virtually the entire wild population of California condors has historically congregated on the Hudson Ranch in late summer and early fall. (No one is sure about the reason for this, but there is some speculation — given that the gathering occurs just before breeding season — that the condors' purpose at the convention is mate selection.) Since broad, open foraging grounds within range of inaccessible mountain retreats are among condors' essential survival requirements, the Condor Research Center, invoking the California Environmental Quality Act, requested an environmental impact report for the proposed development. The developers declined to provide one. Congress then allocated $8.9 million to buy the Hudson Ranch and surrounding property and create a wildlife refuge. The developers declined the government's offer for their share of the property, even though they had defaulted on their payments in three of the years that had passed since the transfer — a fact which, in August 1986, resulted in the property's ownership reverting to the Hudsons. Agricultural real estate values had, in the meantime, fallen off sharply; and on December 31, 1986, the U.S. Fish and Wildlife Service finally bought the Hudson Ranch for $3.5 million. It now makes up the bulk of the Bitter Creek National Wildlife Refuge.

Meanwhile, Tenneco West is planning open oil and toxic waste disposal ponds on the nearby San Emidio Ranch. Condors cannot distinguish between oil and water. Two of eleven captive-raised Andean condors, released to the wild, were found stuck in a stream containing oil effluents. One of the most numerous of the 133 species of bird fossils found in the La Brea tar pits is that of *Gymnogyps amplus,* the prehistoric condor.

A few miles beyond the sign for Los Padres National Forest, we came to a campground called Valle Vista, where a Coors can came flying from a pickup full of hunters. Eric made a disparaging remark. Eben said, "They're to be pitied, not blamed. They can't think. All they understand is privilege." We descended the dirt road to the campground — a broad shelf dotted with piñon pines above a plunging canyon. The drizzle had let up, but we were now more than 4,000 feet above sea level, and low white clouds obscured parts of the surrounding ridges. Where there weren't any clouds, I could see steep hillsides merging washes of green, yellow, brown, and olive. Eric got out of the car and walked around saying, "This is a great campsite. Yes sir, this is a good one." Despite the utter quietness of the place, he spoke at a volume appropriate to transmission over distances.

We needed firewood, so before it got dark the three of us set out searching for it. A short distance from the campground, the hillside dropped away precipitously. Climbing down it was easy; climbing back up with arms full of firewood was rather more inconvenient. The earth was soft, loamy. There were plenty of good-sized branches scattered around, but Eric insisted on chopping a fallen tree trunk in two and dragging half of it back up the hill. Eben said that the canyon below us represented yet another somnolent section of the San Andreas Fault.

When we returned to the campsite, we found that our party had begun to expand; waiting for us were two men from Modesto, Paul Illick and Don Kneiss. One was a contractor, the other a junior college counselor; both were Stanislaus Audubon members whom Eric had invited with the intent of "radicalizing" them. Gradually, other people trickled in too: David Phillips, the wildlife programs coordinator for Friends of the Earth in San Francisco; Keith Axelson, a graphic designer from L.A. with a car full of camera lenses that looked like bazookas; Dee Allen, a doctoral candidate in Renaissance biography who turned out to be the high school friend who had gotten Eric interested in birds at Sequoia.

A chilling fog had come in around the campsite. Axelson, a dapper-looking man with a white mustache that turns up at the corners, already appeared to be growing homesick for the heat of the L.A. basin. "This is a great place, Eben," he offered with a generous helping of sarcasm.

"Well, I'd rather be here than down where you live," Eben answered.

"Keith has a new eight-hundred-millimeter lens," said Eric, peering through the rear window of Axelson's VW squareback.

"Maybe now he'll get a good picture," said Eben. "By golly, Keith took a photograph of a deer walking through an oat field — I think every ranch in this country has a better one on the wall, but it won first prize in a magazine contest."

Eric decided to cook up a few things — specifically hot dogs and, for a beverage, "Postum," a nauseating brew of bran, wheat, and molasses of which Eben is much enamored. This idea in itself was unfortunate, but Eric subsequently tried to achieve it by using charcoal briquettes: he placed a cinderblock on top of the camp grill, filled one of the cavities with charcoal, and doused the cache with lighter fluid. It occurred to me that, even if he managed to make it burn, it would take at least half an hour to get going and then we would still be freezing, with no fire. So I collected some of our wood, which, having been rained on for most of the day, mightily resisted my efforts to ignite it while everyone stood around watching. Finally Eben observed, "I can see that David wouldn't be much use in the Arctic."

"What am I doing wrong, Eben?"

"Well, you need a flame."

He picked up a long limb and tried to break it by bashing it on another log. "Let's see if I can hit that thing where it won't bounce," he said, gratifying the rest of us with his futility. Finally Axelson grabbed the limb and smashed it on the edge of a 55-gallon drum; half the branch jetted into the can, which somehow struck all of us as hilarious. Several short whistle bursts sounded nearby, and Eric said, "What's that, Eb?"

"Screech owl," answered Eben.

"Would he respond to a pygmy owl?"

"He might."

Eben and Eric walked off into the fog, their voices rising, calling out, and drifting back to us after they'd disappeared. I commented to the others that, in Eben's presence, Eric seemed to be imitating aspects of the older man's personality.

Axelson said, "I think we all do."

The first California condor removed from the wild for the purpose of captive breeding was taken on August 13, 1982. The bird was a nestling; the scientists said that its parents had been feeding it irregularly. The chick would go three or four days without food, the recovery team would request permission from the state fish and game commission to capture it, permission would be refused, and then the parents would return and feed the nestling. Finally the scientists were allowed to take the chick. They found that it weighed thirteen pounds — not an alarmingly low figure for a bird of its age — and that it was a male.

When, a few months later, the recovery team asked to capture another condor, the commission stipulated that it be a female. The bird was to be held only long enough to determine its sex through blood analysis; if it proved to be a male, it was to be released. The recovery team trapped another free-flying condor in early December of the same year; lab tests showed that it was a male. But then the weather took a nasty turn, and the scientists said that releasing the condor might endanger it. After a couple of days went by, it was announced that the captive bird had lost weight; it was taken to Los Angeles for feeding and observation. After a week there it gained back the weight, but zoo veterinarians said that it might now have aspergillosis, a mold fungus disease. The bird remained in captivity. The Christmas holidays came and went. So did the scientists. In early January, the recovery team requested permission to keep the condor permanently; after a month in captivity, they said, the bird was too tame to be released. Permission was granted.

Now, as we sat in the dark by our finally burning fire, Eric said of the first captive condor: "Eb, Ogden told me that the week before they took the chick, its parents had been in there feeding it every day."

"Is that right!" Eben said. "The newspaper stories made it sound like they were rescuing it."

"Well, they convinced me at the hearing that they needed to rescue it," Eric said.

"People have been saying for as long as I can remember that we ought to feed condors," said Eben. "But in nature, one specie never feeds another! With any animal, if you take them away and sort of subsidize them, they become dependent on you in no time a'tall. Nature has built strength into the system through adversity; animals need to fend for themselves. One of the real vital experiences in survival is learning how to forage. Now, in the case of the condor, where even the wild birds can't survive, is it fair to ask birds raised in cages to try it? I wouldn't have any argument with captive breeding if they'd explored the other avenues first — if they'd investigated poisons and hunting. But they're doing the last phase first. It's like building a barn and starting with the roof."

"But there's some urgency to this, Eben," said a voice from across the fire. "There's a sense that, if we wait, the condors might be all gone."

"But you've got to look back to 1967," Eben answered. "That's how long these things should have been happening. In our study, my brother and I found five condor carcasses, and three of them were associated with 1080 poison. And we were just going out on weekends over a period of two years; sometimes we didn't get into the field for a month. But people in the Condor Recovery Program never found anything. I don't think they'd find an elephant if you wheeled it right out in front of them. There are a lot of things to find out right now that I could hire a guy from the local service station to just go out and do. One condor died right down in this canyon here, and the recovery team laid the blame on a cyanide coyote-getter. The thing that gripes me is that the recovery people were right up above and didn't even know that this guy was down there poisoning coyotes. If you hired somebody to look after cattle like that, you'd have to tell 'em to get on down the road. Twice I've had badgers come in and die right after they put out poison; coyotes and canine species are more susceptible to 1080 than scavengers, but to this day they don't know how much 1080 it'd take to kill a condor."

"Isn't 1080 illegal?" someone asked.

"If you think that matters, you don't know California," said somebody else. "DDT is being used right now in the Central Valley. They have to smuggle it up from Mexico, but they use it.* I read recently that 1080 was being used illegally on William P. Clark's ranch."

"They use it to kill ground squirrels," Eben said, "but those are too big for a condor to swallow whole. I think the culprit is kangaroo rats. I examined some that had been poisoned, and the average pouch content was twenty-one grains; one of them had thirty-four. I think two of those would kill an elephant. I talked to a cowboy once who said he'd seen

* In 1986, a condor egg collapsed under the weight of its incubating parent; on inspection, the shell was found to be 60 percent thinner than normal, and its membrane contained 180 parts per million of DDE, the residual breakdown product of DDT.

condor competing along the line to swallow poisoned kangaroo rats. The guy who was running the poisoning program on the Tejon Ranch told me that condors got to anticipating where the crew would be from one day to the next; the birds would be sitting there in the trees, waiting for them to poison the squirrels."

Eric poked at the fire and nodded. "I find out more in casual conversation in this country than I ever have from the research," he said.

"That's always true of any research," said Eben. "You never know when you'll meet a guy who came around a bend and saw two condor on a coyote carcass. That was an advantage of Koford's — he had the complete confidence of people in the region. They'd serve as his eyes when he was away."

Eric said, "People seem to think the condors aren't here if they don't see any."

"That's one of the weak points in the program," said Eben. "They only put stock in positive information. Negative information is just as important. The way a bird acts when you're around is no indication of what it's going to do six, or twenty-four, or forty-eight hours later. This was something Koford brought out — the delayed-response phenomenon. The birds would react to some disturbance a long time after it happened. They might be roosting in a tree and some guy would drive some cattle through below them, and the condors would just sit there. But the next day they wouldn't come back. Even though he'd seen them using that tree as a roost every day for a week, they never came back to use it again after that. With a bird like the condor, even a year's worth of data isn't significant at all; they might do one thing one year and then do the opposite thing the next. We used to see them steadily around my place when they used it as a feeding ground; then a year or two would go by when you didn't see them at all; then they'd be back the year after that. It takes a long time to gather information on condors, but the recovery team doesn't want to wait; their goal is captive breeding. I think it's been their goal from the beginning."

"Captive breeding has lots of rewards for investigators," said one of the others. "It has sex appeal. The thing without sex appeal is to stop people from killing condors."

Eben said, "Yes. And that's much harder, because then you're working with people. The average person doesn't pay attention; if a condor lit on their house, they might think it was a turkey. Those of us who are interested in nature need to act as watchdogs. Snyder and Ogden are tinkerers, not environmentalists. Koford was the kind of scientist who could hold the whole picture together in his head, but there are a lot of 'ecologists' who don't really understand ecology. Snyder and Ogden know as much about grass as a hound dog knows about law. The first time I talked to them, they were like children; they had no concept at all of what was going on on the ranges here — the climatic changes, the fluctuations of plants, why cattle feed on one side of the hill at this time of year and the other side of the hill at another. You've got to pretty near live in this country to understand the problems."

"If you look at this area, it's not just the condor," Eric said. "It's the whole ecosystem. It's the kit fox, the alligator lizard . . ."

"I can tell you three birds in the condor range right now that would still be in trouble even if we saved the condor," said Eben. "The blue grosbeak, the yellow-bellied cuckoo, and the Swainson hawk. I remember when you could see ten thousand Swainson hawks migrating across the Carrisa Plains in the spring, but I haven't seen a single one in the last ten years."

"The condor is like the jaguar in Central America," said

someone else. "The animal is endangered. So is the habitat."

Eben said, "My argument has always been that even if we sacrificed the condor trying to save it in the wild, we'd learn things that would help us to save other species in the future. We have something to learn by trying to preserve condors in the wild. We don't have anything to learn by preserving them in a zoo."

The zoo note in the condor cacophony has recently swelled in pitch to the point where many now consider it to be the dominant strain in the score. The so-called zoo wars began when the San Diego Wild Animal Park was designated as the recovery program's official captive breeding site and received $170,000 from the federal government to build the first "condorminiums." This selection didn't sit well with the Los Angeles Zoo, which since 1967 had been the home of the only California condor in captivity: Topa-Topa, captured as an undernourished juvenile after apparently being deserted by its parents. Moreover, the L.A. Zoo has always suffered from comparisons with its San Diego counterpart. A visit to Washington, D.C., and to the secretary of the interior, James Watt, was subsequently paid by the president of the Greater Los Angeles Zoo Association, Marcia Hobbs — who also happens to be the daughter of William A. Wilson, then special envoy to the Vatican, and the goddaughter of one Ronald Reagan. Soon after Mrs. Hobbs's trip, the L.A. Zoo was designated as a second condor breeding site, and an agreement was drawn up governing the allocation of birds and eggs between San Diego and Los Angeles.

Originally, the recovery plan had called for the capture of nine wild condors in order to establish five captive breeding pairs (including Topa-Topa). Some of their offspring were to be released to join the existing wild population; the ultimate goal was to establish a self-sustaining population of at least a hundred birds. In 1980 it was still unknown whether California condors would, like their South American cousins, "double-clutch" — that is, lay a replacement egg if their first one disappeared. This question was answered in 1981, when the egg of a nesting pair of condors in Los Angeles County was knocked from a cave and smashed. After finding another nest site — a significant instinctual detail, as it apparently indicates some understanding on the part of the birds as to the unsuitability of the first — the female condor laid a second egg. At hearings before the state fish and game commission in March of 1983, opponents of the recovery program argued that this new evidence of double-clutching eliminated the necessity of removing hatched condors from the wild; if a breeding pair's first egg were taken and the second left alone, a captive flock could be created without expense to the wild population.

However, at the same hearing Warren Thomas, the director of the L.A. Zoo, proposed taking all first-clutch eggs *plus* the second egg or nestling. "It is in the best interests of the bird to push the bird to its maximum potential," Thomas declared. The Fish and Wildlife Service then asked the commission to double the captive flock to twenty. Four condor eggs were removed from caves in 1983; six more were taken in 1984. In 1985, the number of California condors in zoos surpassed the number in the wild.

One of the reasons the scientists give for taking so many condors into captivity is the importance of maintaining genetic diversity in the species, and hence averting the inbreeding "bottleneck" that produces weak offspring in a small, isolated population. Blood enzyme tests have recently indicated, however, that genetic diversity in the condor may already be as low as 1 percent. Despite the ongoing appropriation of condor eggs and chicks, DNA mitochondrial studies have never been conducted on the condor population; so it's still not known, for example, whether half the entire captive breeding stock might be the progeny of a pair of sisters — a genetically narrow state of affairs that would not be broadened no matter how many condors were hatched in captivity.

"Some species maintain their diversity through something other than genes," Eben posited as our campfire dwindled to a glow. "Some — the peregrine, the gyr falcon, the condor — have always been rare. I think the real reason the L.A. Zoo wants condors is because it can't afford a Chinese panda. If they have a condor, they might be able to work out a trade."

There was chuckling in the darkness, but Eben wasn't joking. "Zoo people are just like cigar store clerks," he said. "They'll buy anything, and they'll sell cheap. They don't promote animals as part of the environment; they can't. An animal in a zoo is just a cross between a wild animal and one that's stuffed. Try getting some information at the L.A. Zoo. It's all promotional; they have to sell their operation as good and proper in order to have a job and seem important. Even with endangered species, you're not told what you're doing wrong, only what the zoo is doing right. Zoos are circus sideshows, and the people who run them are barkers."

Now we are driving back down Mount Pinos, having been rained out on the summit. The road winds along the spine of the mountain; the country is ivory-colored, with gray-green vegetation: juniper, scrub oak, and piñon pine seeming simultaneously haggard and hardy in the hard-baked earth. We pass the Pine Mountain Auto Center, the area's only outpost of civilization — a grocery and gas complex flying the American flag across the road from a golf course surrounded by Swiss-style chalets. Gazing at the fairways, Eben says, "God, that green is vivid! It look like a psychedelic scene." Lower on the mountain the rain is reduced to a drizzle, then stops altogether; finally, to our amazement, the sun comes out, illuminating a golden network of hills to the north, outlined and etched with deep black shadows. To the south are craggy, plummeting ridges. Wherever dirt tracks depart from the main road, hunters' pickups are parked.

"Getting a deer here is a million-to-one jackpot," says Eben. "Down in L.A., the gunstore owners show these guys pictures and say, 'Oh, yeah, there's a lot of deer up there!' If you pursued it, you could almost have a case of misrepresentation. Some of these guys rent a gun and buy a few boxes of shells, and they don't want to have any ammunition left; if they don't get a deer they get desperate, and they start shooting those shells off. On Saturday and Sunday afternoons it sounds just like a little war going on."

We pass by our campground at Valle Vista. A couple of miles farther is the Los Padres National Forest sign, surrounded now by cars and people. The cars are laden with equipment: cameras, lenses, tripods, telescopes. One license plate says BIRDIN. The people — there are at least a dozen representing all age groups; some are from our previous night's party, and some are not — wear blue jeans, parkas, and sweatshirts decorated with drawings of bats, pandas, and hummingbirds. One white-haired man's jacket is covered with sewn-on patches that say SAMBURU KENYA, LA DIGUE SEYCHELLES, KICHWA TEMBO, MASAI MARA, and O'REILLY'S GREEN MOUNTAIN, VERMONT. His younger companion, looking through field glasses, says, "How about a Hutton's vireo?"

"Could be. That's not the way they behave very much, though."

"Is that a Brewer's sparrow?"

"Immature junco. Oh, here — possible chipping sparrow on tree. About eye level."

Eben's entrance onto the scene as usual stimulates a minor

stir. He is the eccentric old man, the colorful sage, the back-country guru. His effect on this group of amateur naturalists is that of a magnet on iron filings. As people greet him he grins amiably, shaking various right hands with his left. One man says, "This is my fourth trip down here and I haven't seen a condor yet."

Eben says, "Well, you'll see one today."

"You heard him," the man tells the others.

The view from this lookout offers a roadside panorama of condor country, a powerful dose of the immensity of America. Steep red and white cliffs descend from both right and left to frame a section of dull brown foothills, gentle in comparison with the cliffs. There are distant dirt roads and cattle trails traversing the tops of open ridges, and immense brown sandstone rocks in the middle of the landscape. Beyond these hills stretches the San Joaquin Valley, a flat quilt of green and brown squares — those that are irrigated and those that are plowed. Away to the northwest the hills go white, or almost pink, like tortured flesh — the southern end of the Temblors, a forbidding no man's land that appears to be suffocating in some sort of haze. To the southeast, the Tehachapis are faintly blue on the horizon when they're visible at all; the fitful storm clouds come and go, obscuring sections of the entire picture, occasionally reducing our field of vision to the bare brown hillsides immediately before us.

Some of the people perched on the lookout are zoology students from Cal Poly, San Luis Obispo, who are helping the recovery team keep track of condors. They are well equipped and girded for the day with powerful spotting scopes, coolers full of soft drinks and sandwiches, and umbrellas to protect them from both rain and sun. They report that they've already seen two condors this morning, in the vicinity of Oak Knoll. Condor watchers have divided this landscape into its visual components and assigned each a

name: Oak Knoll, Lone Tree, S-Road, Left Ridge, Brush
Mountain. The landmarks serve as communication aids in
the task of locating the birds. To wit, Eric, looking through
his field glasses, now says, "Sight down to Lone Tree. Above
that — about three quarters of a field of binoculars — there's
a bunch of ravens with something big cutting through the
middle of them. I think it's an eagle."

Eben sets about fulfilling his function: "A golden eagle has
sharp pointed wings that are wide at the wrist. They cut
back in near the body to make a wedge of space. A condor's
wings come right to the body with no space there. Just when
a condor is ready to head out, he'll dip those wings and go
into his flex-glide. When his wings catch the air, it sounds
like a flute. If he thought you were a carcass, he'd come down
and play you a little tune. Keep your eye out for turkey vultures; if a condor is in the area, he'll join them because he
knows they're riding the thermals. A turkey vulture will tip
in the wind, but a condor is heavy enough to where he'll stay
in the same plane. An awful lot of people mistake condors for
airplanes because they're so stable. The larger the soaring
bird, the bigger the circle it makes. If the gyrations last
twelve to fifteen seconds, that would probably be a golden
eagle. Under twelve, you drop down to a Cooper's hawk.
Anything over fifteen seconds should arouse your suspicion."

At eleven A.M. not much is stirring. An elderly lady in a pink
and white Hawaiian shirt says, "What's that down there in
the bush? Is it an eagle?"

Looking through his binoculars, Eric says, "No. It's a redtailed hawk."

"But it has a golden head."

"No, it's gray," says Eric. "It has a pale breast and its
shoulders aren't very broad. An eagle has a dark breast."

"*Shoot,*" says the lady. "I knew it would turn out to be a redtail. It always does."

"What's that on the ground below Lone Tree?" somebody asks.

Eric says, "That's a cow."

Noon. Eric announces, "There's a pair of condor at five o'clock. They're circling. They're gonna get up above the horizon in about thirty seconds." He looks at his watch, then back at the black dots in the distance. "They just hit. Took 'em eighteen seconds."

"Where are you talking about?"

"In the flat beyond Lone Tree there's a red and white tower. Not the Purina one, though. Above it there's a line of white clouds superimposed on the gray. The birds are just to the right of it."

"Oh, yeah!"

"Oh, they're huge!"

"Those are condor," Eric says. "Two adults."

"I just lost them over Brush Mountain."

Eric says, "They'll be back, and they might be close."

One P.M. The rain returns. Seeking shelter, I squat in the side door of a Chevy van that two short-haired, mustachioed men have driven up from L.A. They have brought a whole batch of printed material — not many bird books to speak of, but rather the Sunday *Los Angeles Times.* I ask to see the Calendar section. "Sure," one of the young men says with an accent that sounds vaguely British. Then, brandishing a plastic pitcher, he asks: "Fancy a Bloody Mary?"

Two P.M. A cow and a calf are seen galloping across Oak Knoll. One of the elderly ladies says, "Look at those cattle running! Oh, they're going so fast!"

"There's a pair of eagles above them," says Eben. "They must have scared those cattle. There's no authentic record of eagles ever killing them, though. I saw an article in *The Condor* that said a golden eagle had killed a calf; how this was published in the name of scientific evidence I'll never know. I guess somebody came around a bend and saw an eagle eating on a calf that was still moving. Well, in my life I've seen that dozens of times. In winter, if a calf is born deformed and unable to bleat or blather, I've seen three or four eagles standing around waiting for the old cow to leave. The cow goes off, comes back, goes off; after a while it loses its protective attitude. Then again, sometimes you'll see a condor feeding on a dead calf and the old cow will make a run at it."

A couple of ravens come shooting through the space in front of us, their wings inclined backward like jet planes'. "Ravens just seem to enjoy flying," Eben observes.

Three o'clock marks the arrival of John Ogden, the Audubon Society's biologist in the Condor Recovery Program. His blue jeans are held up by a belt with an owl in the buckle, and his short-sleeve khaki shirt has an Audubon patch on the shoulder. Like actors playing Tarzan, condor biologists have come and gone over the years, each bringing a different character and type of musculature to the job. Fred Sibley, the first person to fill the position, was known as an aggressive field man who visited, entered, measured, and photographed 27 condor nests in 1966 and 1967. (Interestingly, the year after this series of invasions, he found only one.) He was followed by Dean Carrier, a humorous sort who liked to play practical jokes on his colleagues, composing letters from fictional correspondents reporting condors in places where they were not known to exist. Carrier also wrote the Forest Service management plan upon which the Condor Recovery Plan was based. Sanford Wilbur was the first condor biologist to espouse captive breeding and radiotelemetry; more theorist than field biologist, he hypothesized that there were two condor populations — one in the Sierra Nevada and one in the Coast Range — and that the birds were having problems reproducing. Both theories turned out to be wrong.

When they came to the condor program, John Ogden and Noel Snyder — the Fish and Wildlife condor biologist — seemed like peas in a pod. Both were the same age, forty-one; both had the same amount of gray in their beards; both came to California from Florida, where they had distinguished themselves working with other endangered species. Ogden had banded hundreds of ospreys, fastened more than a thousand wing tags to wood storks, and attached radio transmitters to crocodiles. Trying to find out why wood storks were disappearing, he determined that the draining of marshes and the impounding of water for agriculture had altered the wetlands' natural patterns to such a degree that fish were no longer concentrated enough to constitute an effective food supply. Snyder had worked with Everglade kites and practiced captive breeding on Puerto Rican parrots, which were threatened by the pearly-eyed thrasher, an unwelcome exotic that stabs parrots' babies with its beak. The parrot population had fallen to a total of thirteen individuals; Snyder altered their nest holes to exclude the thrashers, and the parrots made a modest comeback.

In California, Snyder was charged with the study of condor breeding biology, so he oversaw the taking of eggs and chicks. Ogden studied the birds on their foraging range and therefore ran the radiotelemetry program. Ogden was, then, more directly concerned with habitat questions, and he was the first person officially to recommend federal acquisition of the Hudson Ranch. Snyder, an intuitive and creative scientist, developed a photo-censusing technique for identifying individual birds by their molt patterns; he also posited what is now considered a major condor mortality problem: lead poisoning from bullets in deer carcasses. In time, however, he came to believe that it was impossible to preserve condors in the wild, and he focused his attention on building a captive population. Ogden opposed the total-capture approach if for no other reason than that wild birds are instrumental in protecting the habitat for future releases. Impulsive and stubborn, Snyder appears to resent scientific opinions rebutting his own; when his colleagues in the condor program resisted his ideas, he cultivated the zoos and Marcia Hobbs, with whom he is known to have consulted closely and often.*

On other condor watches here, Snyder has remained aloof from any contact with Eben's party. Ogden, by contrast, now chats with the group good-naturedly. When David Brower, who founded Friends of the Earth — one of the most vehement opponents of the Condor Recovery Program — was here two weeks ago getting his first look ever at a condor, Eric took pictures of him eating watermelon and laughing with Ogden. Now Eric snaps one of Ogden and Eben with their arms around each other's shoulders.

Sometimes, it seems to me, Eben is rather soft on his adversaries when confronted with them directly; for someone so harshly critical of his neighbors' lives and attitudes, he's awfully friendly to them when they're around. It was only last night, after all, that he told us Ogden was "a tinkerer, not an

* Both Ogden and Snyder have since left the condor program. In November 1984, Ogden returned to Florida, where he is now director of ornithological research for Audubon. Snyder was recalled to Washington, D.C., by the Fish and Wildlife Service in March 1986, but, on the day he was scheduled to report, he took sick leave for a heart condition; when his leave expired, he resigned from the service (though he continued to participate in condor working-group meetings as Marcia Hobbs's representative). At this writing, the director of the Condor Research Center is Oliver Pattee, a career Fish and Wildlife biologist who has previously studied lead-shot poisoning in bald eagles.

environmentalist." When I ask Eben about this, he says, "I respect a person with an opposing viewpoint unless they're operating on subterfuge. Snyder's always weighing what he says to me — he couches things so he won't have to show his hand. We seldom talk. Ogden knows what's on my mind from meetings; he hasn't answered my questions about poison, so there's no use in us going any further. But if he starts defending what they've done, I'll get involved."

Ogden leaves without defending what the biologists have done.

Four P.M. The air is filled with a gusty drizzle. Someone says, "There's something big above Lone Tree. It's being chased by two smaller birds."

"Condor!" cries Eben. "Flex-glide!"

"What I'm seeing ain't in a flex-glide," says Eric.

"Well," says Eben, "I can't see so good."

"Condor," confirms Eric, studying the speck. "Coming our way."

The bird is cruising in leisurely loops, like a toy boat circling in an eddy. When it enters the foreground below us, still too distant for its white wingpatches to be visible, it turns, banks, and rises. Now it does go into the flex-glide, dipping its wings and suddenly soaring behind the ridge to our left. Having tired of the social scene, I climb the clay embankment on the other side of the road, slip through the barbed-wire fence, and set off in the direction where the condor disappeared.

A warm wind is blowing now; the rain has stopped. I tie my coat around my waist and ascend a hill of oak and foxtail. Beyond the ridge that borders the road is a broad brown and yellow valley with gigantic outcroppings of pockmarked rocks. The surrounding hillsides are bare, eroded; but on the higher hills the bush takes over — green manzanita, chaparral. Behind these foothills four ridges recede, becoming bluer as they grow more distant. There are flat banks of fog in the far valleys and stacks of gray clouds on the horizon. A black dot rises from the ridgeline; I raise my glasses and it leaps into close-up: the condor, its white patches clearly visible against the black, widespread wings.

The bird banks and rises in lazy circles, another smaller raptor behind it, and I realize for the umpteenth time how regal raptors are on their rounds; it has to do with how little effort they seem to expend, how steady their bearing is, how unchallenged their place in the sky. As advertised, this particular condor is steady to the point of an aeronautic appearance; it looks like a glider or Piper Cub with wings supported by solid struts. Nevertheless, the fingerlike pinion feathers seem to express an attitude of relaxedness; they're spread the way your fingers would be if you were shooing something away from you — an air of utter independence.

After a lengthy period of circling, the bird comes to earth on the valley floor, a few hundred yards from a cluster of farm buildings. I watch through the binoculars for a while, but the condor doesn't move, so I keep on hiking. There are lots of brightly colored wildflowers in this barren-looking landscape — purple asters with yellow centers, scarlet buglers being visited by iridescent hummingbirds. I find the big brown rocks in the valley to be filled with caves, and I crawl inside one to get out of the rain — which has, not surprisingly, resumed. Eventually, though, opting for view, I climb the exterior of the cliff in a fine misting shower. When I get to the top, I look up and am startled to see the condor above me.

The bird seems to be scrutinizing me. (I remember Ken Brower's line: "When man and condor meet today, it is with a glance of mutual appraisal, each to see whether the other is yet extinct.") What, I wonder, do you say when you're finally face-to-face with an absolute — the biggest bird in North America, the embodiment of all endangered species, a messenger from the living to the dead. I don't say anything; I stand in the rain with upturned face, a lone earthling rooted to a rock, regarding the hovering form of extinction. This condor is an anomaly, I know: a living incarnation of mortality. Spinning high in the air above me, framed against storm clouds, with warm sheets of water blowing between us, it seems a specter. It occurs to me that this spooky creature has on a hell of a Halloween costume: a skeleton suit and a jack-o'-lantern head, a vivid uniform for a vulture. The decoration alone would set it apart from any other bird, and the temptation to assign it symbolic status is irresistible. But as I watch it, the condor doesn't strike me as a symbol of extinction so much as a totem for North America itself. It's because of the coloring, somehow — red, white, and black is a morbid heraldry for a once-promising continent, a land that's been dying since 1492, a place that harbors the exotics of the earth and in doing so drives its native inhabitants into oblivion.

In spite of this, the condor does not appear gloomy; it seems polite, tolerant, curious. After a moment, having witnessed enough of me and my perambulations, it dips its wings and glides away. I glass it in profile and see the naked head extended, held slightly lower than the rest of the horizontal body in the sulky demeanor of vultures. It disappears in the direction of the lookout, and soon I hear distant, excited voices wafting across the sodden landscape: "Hey!" "Hey!" then a second of silence and, finally, cheers and clapping.

For those of us raised far away from wilderness — in places populated solely by domesticated animals, with untamed ones glimpsed only in books or on television — there's something miraculous about seeing them in the wild. The first time I saw a bear in the woods, I couldn't believe there was something so big that nobody owned, fed, or kept on a leash. The self-sustaining ability of nature seems a marvel, though it's literally the oldest thing in the world. Similarly, seeing the condor here where it "belongs" is simultaneously remarkable and mundane. I was actually surprised by how natural it seemed; there were no trumpets, no soundtrack music, no caustic debate, no fee of admission. The condor seemed unaware of its celebrity or of the controversy that surrounds it. It was just a big black and white bird flying around in a quiet canyon. To be sure, its size and bearing distinguish it from any other animal you might imagine; but, for me, the most extraordinary thing about the condor was the fact that it was free.

Seven P.M. Driving back north through the oil country, the pumps nodding and working like a diligent army of dinosaurs, the rain still falling; the last light is a murky gray-brown. Our headlights illuminate scraggly tumbleweeds lining both sides of the highway. In this desert, rain is an oddity; it almost seems to be washing oil out of the air, creating a precipitate and covering the car with it.

"I was thinking about it, Eben," Eric says as he stares out at the endless acres of oil pumps. "The condor is a bird that never had any predators. As a result, it's gentle, open, unhurried; it has time."

"Time, and a friendly attitude," says Eben. "When that bird came over, it was almost like he was saying, 'Help us out.' "

"When people see it, they just murmur," says Eric. "They start talking to themselves. I think you, or I, or Ogden, or Brower . . . we all have the same feeling about it. We have that in common."

By the time we get to the Bitterwater Road, the last long

stretch leading to Eben's ranch, darkness has fully descended. Ahead in the night, on the side of the road, a white shape appears and, when we get close, takes off from a fencepost. We see the flat, ghostlike face outlined in the shape of a heart, moving back and forth as it flies. "Barn owl," Eben says.

In a moment the event repeats itself: another barn owl takes shape and takes off, then another, and another. "It must be on account of the rain," says Eben. "If there are that many next to the road, think how many are out in the fields." We begin counting the owls as they appear, each one materializing like an apparition that evaporates at our approach. At ten, we're excited. At fifteen, Eben exclaims, "This is a real phenomenon!" I lean forward from the back seat, transfixed. Eric takes on new seriousness now, peering raptorlike over the wheel. "Seventeen! Eighteen! Nineteen!" he cries, his eyes easily the best in the car. We three men are suddenly children, tallying the incidence of some kind of automobile during a long monotonous trip — though the model we're hunting hasn't changed in design for quite a few years and, if we're all lucky, won't.

We finish our count at thirty-two.

"When people ask me why I want to save the condor, I say because it's fun," says Eric. We pull up to Eben's place and see Gladys looking out the window. Once again the rain has stopped.

Eric says, "You know, Eb, I was just thinking about how much I've changed since that first time on Mount Pinos."

"I can see that," Eben says. "And not only has your own life changed, but you've changed the lives of others."

Eric looks away, chewing a toothpick. "You watch, Eben," he says. "Within a year we're going to have this whole state organized in favor of the condor. I can feel it."

Epilogue

IN THE WINTER of 1984–85, four of five known wild breeding pairs broke up when six condors disappeared. Only one of the birds was found; it died from lead poisoning. In the face of this "emergency," the California Fish and Game Commission recommended that all remaining California condors be taken into protective custody. As the maintenance of a wild population had always been deemed important — for the purpose of protecting the habitat against commercial development and reintroducing captive-raised birds to the wild — the U.S. Fish and Wildlife Service at first rejected this advice; it decided to capture three of the six remaining birds and release three others in the spring of 1986.

In December 1985 the USFWS changed its mind. It announced its intention to capture all of the remaining condors and canceled plans to release any in the immediate future.

The National Audubon Society filed suit and won an injunction from a U.S. district court prohibiting any further captures, pending a hearing on the possible consequences of such action.

From the beginning of the Condor Recovery Program, some progeny from captive eggs were intended to be released to the wild, but at this writing, none have been. Some zoo authorities now maintain that introducing new birds into a habitat that has proved lethal would be pointless. In May 1985, five young California condors at the L.A. Zoo earmarked for release were removed from isolation and familiarized with their human handlers instead. No government agency authorized the action; no disciplinary measures resulted.

In June 1986, a federal court of appeals overturned Audubon's injunction against capturing the remaining birds. On Easter Sunday of 1987, the last California condor was taken from the wild.

Acknowledgments
Selected Bibliography
Index

Acknowledgments

Any work of journalism owes its existence to the cooperation of knowledgeable people who, for reasons I don't particularly understand, consent to spend hours talking to a total stranger. In researching this book, I have been privileged to meet scores of amiable experts from many fields in many pleasant settings.

The person who originally introduced me to Eben McMillan and the issues surrounding the California condor was Mark Palmer of the Sierra Club's San Francisco Bay Chapter. He has been an invaluable source of information on environmental topics, as has David Phillips (formerly of Friends of the Earth, now of Earth Island Institute). John Ogden and Linda Blum of the National Audubon Society answered many of my questions about the condor program forthrightly and in detail. Other people from the Condor

Research Center who provided me with information are John Borneman of Audubon, Oliver Pattee and Joseph Dowhan of the U.S. Fish and Wildlife Service, and Noel and Helen Snyder. Randy Perry and Jan Rice of the USFWS shed some light on the inner workings of the Condor Recovery Program for me. Brian Walton of the Santa Cruz Predatory Bird Research Group, David DeSante of the Point Reyes Bird Observatory, Cathleen Cox of the Los Angeles Zoo, and Don Sterner of the San Diego Wild Animal Park helped educate me about captive breeding. David Blankenship of Audubon furnished me with information about whooping cranes, and David Klinger and Dick Moore of the USFWS kept me updated on the status of the Hudson Ranch.

Several professors from the Agricultural Extension Service of the University of California at Davis were helpful. Burgess L. ("Bud") Kay contributed the file of letters on the Temblor grazing controversy. At Davis I also discussed grazing practices with Jim Clawson, starlings with Rex Marsh and William Hamilton, and eucalyptus trees with Bill Davis. Others who taught me about the history and biology of eucalyptus were Nancy Horner of the Golden Gate National Recreation Area, Neal Havlik, John Nichols, and Harlan Kessel of the East Bay Regional Parks District, and John Rosenberg of the Park Management Advisory Committee.

My first exposure to underlying problems in the Mediterranean fruit fly program came from Paul Ehrlich and Bruce Wilcox of the Center for Conservation Biology at Stanford University. Donald Dahlsten of the University of California at Berkeley and Robert Dowell of the Division of Plant Industry in the California Department of Food and Agriculture later gave me an earful on the subject. Robert Metcalf of the Institute for Environmental Studies at the University of Illinois, Margaret Race of the Division of Agriculture and Natural Resources at U.C. Berkeley, Kevin Shay of the East

Bay Regional Parks District, and David Roe of the Environmental Defense Fund also provided me with facts pertaining to the Medfly.

I obtained information about Carl Koford, Joseph Grinnell, and Alden Miller from Steve Herman of Evergreen State College and from Oliver Pearson, Alice Landauer, and Ned Johnson of the U.C. Museum of Vertebrate Zoology at Berkeley. Ward Russell, a retired preparator for that museum, recounted the incident of the condor carcass killing the dermestid beetles. James Parsons of the geography department at U.C. Berkeley talked to me about the Carrizo Plain and loaned me copies of the *Valley Herald*. John Evans of the University of California Extension at San Luis Obispo elucidated agricultural pressures in San Luis Obispo County for me. Sandra Schultz and Robert Wallace of the U.S. Geological Survey educated me about the San Andreas Fault.

For background pertaining to other earthquake faults and the history of the Diablo Canyon nuclear power plant, I consulted Fred Eissler of the Scenic Shoreline Preservation Committee, Mark Evanoff of People for Open Space, Doug Hamilton of Earth Science Associates, Lloyd Cluff of Pacific Gas and Electric, Dick Hubbard of MHB Associates, James Crouch of Crouch, Bachman, and Associates, Stanley Mendes, and Ralph Vrana.

I gained insight into the McMillan family from the late A. Starker Leopold, Dorothy Twisselmann, John Taft, Delia Wegus, Jim Sinton, William Wreden, Margaret Owings, William Penn Mott, and Don, Greg, and Linda McMillan. Eben and Ian's sister Dorothy furnished me with an invaluable hundred-page oral family history compiled by her daughter, Marlis Baloh.

For all manner of information, I am continually obliged to the unsung heroes on the staff of the main branch of the Oakland Public Library.

For various kinds of advice, information, encouragement,

and support, I am indebted to Eric Caine, Carol Cleveland, Lynn Ferrin, Fred Hill, Roger Luckenbach, Suzanne Mantell, John Raeside, Russell Shay, Bill Strachan, and my parents, David and Patricia Darlington.

Last, but obviously not least, I am grateful to Eben, Gladys, Ian, and May McMillan — for their hospitality and for an education that I could never have gotten from anybody else.

Selected Bibliography

Angel, Myron. *La Piedra Pintada — The Painted Rock of California.* Los Angeles: Grafton, 1910.

Berger, Andrew J. "Reintroduction of Hawaiian Geese." In *Endangered Birds,* edited by Stanley A. Temple. Madison: University of Wisconsin Press, 1978.

Bernard de Hautcilly, Auguste. *Duhaut-Cilly's Account of California in the Years 1827–28.* San Francisco: California Historical Society, 1929.

Brautigan, Richard. *A Confederate General from Big Sur.* New York: Grove Press, 1964.

Brower, Kenneth. "The Naked Vulture and the Thinking Ape." *Atlantic Monthly,* October 1983.

Carpenter, E. J., and R. Earl Storie. *Soil Survey of the Paso Robles Area.* Washington, D.C.: U.S. Government Printing Office, 1933.

Carrier, W. Dean. "The California Condor Recovery Plan." *Outdoor California* 44, no. 5 (September–October 1983).

Clark, Jerry P. *Vertebrate Pest Control Handbook.* Sacramento: California Department of Food and Agriculture, 1986.

Conway, William G. "Breeding Endangered Birds in Captivity: The Last Resort." In *Endangered Birds,* edited by Stanley A. Temple. Madison: University of Wisconsin Press, 1978.

Cooke, May Thatcher. *Spread of the European Starling in North America.* Washington, D.C.: U.S. Department of Agriculture Circular No. 336, 1925.

Dahlsten, Donald. "Control of Invaders." In *Ecological Studies, Vol. 58: Ecology of Biological Invasions of North America and Hawaii,* edited by Harold A. Mooney and James A. Drake. New York: Springer-Verlag, 1986.

————. Editorial in *Environment* 23 (October 1981).

————. "Pesticides in an Era of Integrated Pest Management." *Environment* 25 (December 1983): 45–54.

Dasmann, Raymond F. *The Destruction of California.* New York: Macmillan, 1965.

Davis, John. "In Memoriam: Alden Holmes Miller." *The Auk* 84 (April 1967): 192–202.

DeTreville, Susan. "Coping with Cougars." *Defenders,* January–February 1985.

Dreistadt, Steve H., and Donald L. Dahlsten. "California's Medfly Campaign: Lessons from the Field." *Environment* 28 (July–August 1986): 18–20.

Dugdale, Peggy. "Cash Meltdown at Diablo Canyon." *San Francisco Magazine,* February 1984.

Eakin, Richard M., A. Starker Leopold, and Ruben A. Stirton. "Alden Holmes Miller 1906–1965" (memorial epitaph).

Eichel, Marjean H. "The Carrizo Plain: A Geographic Study of Land Use, Settlement, and Change." Master's thesis in geography, San Jose State University, June 1971.

Evanoff, Mark. "Boondoggle at Diablo: The 18-Year War Against Truth." *Not Man Apart* 11 (September 1981): D1–16.

Fillip, Janice. "Saving the California Condor." *California Living / San Francisco Examiner,* June 29, 1980.

Fisher, Walter K. "When Joseph Grinnell and I Were Young." *The Condor* 42 (January–February 1940): 35–38.

Fox, Stephen. *John Muir and His Legacy: The American Conservation Movement.* Boston: Little, Brown, 1981.

Fyfe, Richard W. "Reintroducing Endangered Birds to the Wild." In *Endangered Birds,* edited by Stanley A. Temple. Madison: University of Wisconsin Press, 1978.

Garmon, Linda. "Coyote Poison: To Have or Have Not." *Science News* 122 (October 16, 1982): 248–249.

Gilmore, J. E. Introduction to Symposium: "The Medfly in California: The Threat, Defense Strategies, and Public Policy." *Hort-Science* 18 (February 1983).

Golden, Frederic. "Black Friday, Then Brown Rot." *Time,* August 31, 1981.

Graham, Henry Grey. *The Social Life of Scotland in the Eighteenth Century.* London: A. & C. Black, 1937.

Grinnell, Hilda Wood. "Joseph Grinnell: 1877–1939." *The Condor* 42 (January 1940): 3–18.

Hoagland, Edward. "Hailing the Elusory Mountain Lion." In *Walking the Dead Diamond River.* New York: Random House, 1978.

Holing, Dwight. "Big Cats at Bay." *Defenders,* January–February 1985.

Houston, James D. *Californians: Searching for the Golden State.* New York: Knopf, 1982.

Howard, Walter E. "The European Starling in California." *Bulletin of the California Department of Agriculture* 48 (July–August–September 1959): 171–179.

Jackson, D. S., and Lee, B. G. "Medfly in California 1980–1982." *Bulletin of the Entomological Society of America* 31 (Winter 1985): 29–37.

Johnson, Ron J., and James F. Glahn. "Starlings." *Prevention and Control of Wildlife Damage.* Lincoln: Cooperative Extension Service, Institute of Agriculture and Natural Resources, University of Nebraska, 1983.

Jones, Robert A. "Environmental Movement — Wholesale Changes at Top."*Los Angeles Times,* December 27, 1984 (I:3).

Jurek, Ron. "Giant Bird Faces Giant Problems of Survival." *Outdoor California* 44, no. 5 (September–October 1983).

Kalmbach, E. R. "Winter Starling Roosts of Washington." *Wilson Bulletin* (published by the Wilson Ornithological Society) 44, no. 2 (June 1932): 65–75.

Kessel, Brina. "Distribution and Migration of the European Starling in North America." *The Condor* 55 (March–April 1953): 49–65.

Kiff, Lloyd. "An Historical Perspective on the Condor." *Outdoor California* 44, no. 5 (September–October 1983).

Koford, Carl. *The California Condor.* Research Report No. 4 of the National Audubon Society. New York: National Audubon Society, 1953.

―――. "The Welfare of the Puma in California." *Carnivore I(1).*

Seattle: Carnivore Research Institute, Burke Museum, University of Washington, 1978.

Krauthammer, C. "Brownian Motion." *New Republic,* August 1–8, 1981.

Lanson, Jacqueline Anna. "Eucalyptus in California: Its Distribution, History, and Economic Value." Master's thesis in geography, University of California at Berkeley, 1952.

Lorraine, Hilary, and Derrell L. Chambers. "Eradication of Exotic Species: Recent Experiences in California." In *World Crop Pests: Fruit Flies — Biology, Natural Enemies, and Control,* edited by A. Robinson and G. Hooper. In press.

Mansfield, Terry M. "Mountain Lion Management in California." Paper submitted to the 51st North American Wildlife and Natural Resources Conference, Reno, Nevada, on behalf of the California Department of Fish and Game, Sacramento, California. March 1986.

Marshall, Eliot. "Man Versus Medfly: Some Tactical Blunders." *Science* 213 (July 24, 1981): 417–418.

Matthiessen, Peter. *Wildlife in America.* New York: Viking Press, 1959.

McClintock, Elizabeth. "Ernest Christian Twisselmann (1917–1972)." *Fremontia* I, no. 1 (April 1973): 3–4.

McGuane, Thomas. "Roping from A to B." In *An Outside Chance.* New York: Farrar, Straus, and Giroux, 1980.

McMillan, Ian. "Doing Away with Wildness." *Defenders of Wildlife News,* October–November–December 1968.

———. "Do Whooping Cranes Lay Too Many Eggs?" *Defenders of Wildlife News,* April–May–June 1970.

———. "How to Become a Real Conservationist," *Defenders of Wildlife News,* July–August–September 1969.

———. *Man and the California Condor.* New York: Dutton, 1968.

———. "Of Condors, Kit Foxes, and Compound 1080." *Not Man Apart* 15 (October 1985): 10–11.

McNulty, Faith. "Last Days of the Condor?" *Audubon,* March 1978 and May 1978.

Metcalf, Robert L. "Changing Role of Insecticides in Crop Protection." *Annual Review of Entomology* 25 (1980): 210–256.

Meyer, Jennifer. "To Save the Condor." *Outdoor California* 44, no. 5 (September–October 1983).

Miller, Alden H. "Joseph Grinnell." *Systematic Zoology* 13 (December 30, 1964): 235–242.

Miller, Alden H., Ian I. McMillan, and Eben McMillan. *The Current Status and Welfare of the California Condor.* Research Report No. 6 of the National Audubon Society. New York: National Audubon Society, 1965.

————. "Hope for the California Condor." *Audubon,* January–February 1965.

Miller, Loye. "Notes on Alden Miller." Address at memorial service for Alden H. Miller at the National Academy of Science.

Munz, Philip. *A California Flora.* Berkeley: University of California Press, 1968.

Nelson, J. W., W. C. Dean, and E. C. Eckmann. *Reconnaissance Soil Survey of the Upper San Joaquin Valley.* Washington, D.C.: U.S. Government Printing Office, 1917.

1986 Industrial Outlook. Washington, D.C.: U.S. Government Printing Office, 1986.

Ornduff, Robert. *An Introduction to California Plant Life.* Berkeley: University of California Press, 1974.

Palmer, Mark J. "Cougars on the Run in California." *Pacific Discovery,* January–March 1986.

Parfit, Michael. "Its Days as a Varmint Are Over but the Cougar Is Still on the Run." *Smithsonian,* September 1985.

Phillips, David, and Hugh Nash, ed. *The Condor Question.* San Francisco: Friends of the Earth, 1981.

Pryor, L. D. "Tree of the Future." *American Forests* 73 (February 1967): 12–15.

Redmond, Tim. "The PG&E Papers." *San Francisco Bay Guardian,* November 27–December 4, 1985.

Reed, Nathaniel P., and Dennis Drabelle. *The United States Fish and Wildlife Service.* Boulder: Westview Press, 1984.

Reese, M., et al. "Jerry Brown's War of the Flies." *Newsweek,* July 20, 1981.

————. "March of the Medfly." *Newsweek,* July 27, 1981.

Ritter, William E. "Joseph Grinnell." *Science* 90, no. 2326 (July 28, 1939): 75–76.

Rodale, Robert. "The 1981 Medfly Battle." *Organic Gardening,* September 1981.

Rosetta, Neal. "Herds, Herds on the Range." *Sierra,* March–April 1985.

Sandvig, Earl. "A Fair Price for Privilege." *Sierra,* March–April 1985.

Scribner, Jerry. "The Medfly in California: Organization of the

Eradication Program and Public Policy." *HortScience* 18 (February 1983).

Sears, Paul F. *Deserts on the March.* Norman: University of Oklahoma Press, 1980.

Sheridan, David F. *Desertification of the United States.* Washington, D.C.: Council on Environmental Quality, 1981.

Shrag, Peter. "The California Fruit Fly Wars." *The Nation,* 233 (October 10, 1981): 339–340.

Sitton, Larry W., Sue Allen, Richard A. Weaver, and Wallace G. MacGregor. *California Mountain Lion Study.* Sacramento: The Resources Agency, California Department of Fish and Game, 1976.

Small, Arnold. *The Birds of California.* New York: Winchester Press, 1974.

Smith, Dick. *Condor Journal.* Santa Barbara: Capra Press and the Santa Barbara Museum of Natural History, 1978.

Smith, Gar. "Science Fails the Condor." *This World / San Francisco Examiner,* February 23, 1986.

Snyder, Noel F., and John D. Taapken. "Puerto Rican Parrots and Nest Predation by Pearly-eyed Thrashers." In *Endangered Birds,* edited by Stanley A. Temple. Madison: University of Wisconsin Press, 1978.

Standard and Poor's Industry Surveys. New York: Standard and Poor's Corporation, April 1986.

Steinhardt, Peter. "Does Anyone Know Anything About Mountain Lions?" *Pacific Discovery,* January–March 1986.

Stivens, Dal. "The Roving Eucalypt." *American Forests* 68 (February 1962): 30–31.

Storer, Tracy I., and Lloyd P. Tevis. *The California Grizzly.* Berkeley: University of California Press, 1955.

Temple, Stanley A. "The Concept of Managing Endangered Birds." In *Endangered Birds,* edited by Stanley A. Temple. Madison: University of Wisconsin Press, 1978.

"Those Flies in Brown's Ointment." *Time,* July 29, 1981.

"The Trees that Captured California." *Sunset,* August 1956.

Turbak, Gary. "The Cougar's New Cloak." *National Wildlife,* April–May 1982.

USDA Agricultural Statistics 1985. Washington, D.C.: U.S. Government Printing Office, 1985.

Wallis, Claudia. "Trying to Thwart the Fruit Fly." *Time,* July 27, 1981.

Walsh, John. "Medfly Continues to Bug California." *Science* 214 (December 1981): 1221–1224.

Wilbur, Sanford R., DeLoy Esplin, Robert D. Mallette, John C. Borneman, and William H. Radtkey. *California Condor Recovery Plan.* Washington, D.C.: U.S. Fish and Wildlife Service, January 1980.

Yount, Lisa. "The Fly in our Fruit." *International Wildlife,* November–December 1981.

Zierold, John. "The Medfly, A Mist of Confusion." *Sierra,* November–December 1981.

Zimmerman, David. *To Save a Bird in Peril.* New York: Coward, McCann, and Geoghegan, 1970, 1971, 1972, 1973, 1974, 1975.

Index